KU-252-713

dear annie

dear annie

a no-nonsense guide to getting dressed

Annalisa Barbieri

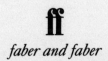

faber and faber

First published in 1998
by Faber and Faber Limited
3 Queen Square London WC1N 3AU
This edition published in 2000

Typeset by Faber and Faber Ltd
Printed in England by Mackays of Chatham plc, Chatham, Kent

All rights reserved

dear annie is a registered trademark

© Annalisa Barbieri, 1998
www.dearannie.com

Annalisa Barbieri is hereby identified as author
of this work in accordance with Section 77
of the Copyright, Designs and Patents Act 1988

*This book is sold subject to the condition that it shall not,
by way of trade or otherwise, be lent, resold, hired out or otherwise
circulated without the publisher's prior consent in any form
of binding or cover other than that in which it is published and
without a similar condition including this condition
being imposed on the subsequent purchaser*

A CIP record for this book
is available from the British Library

ISBN 0-571-20772-3

2 4 6 8 10 9 7 5 3 1

My posture is akin to Neanderthal woman's. Despite repeated – and increasingly fractious – childhood instructions to stand/sit straight, my shoulders' favourite position is still The Stoop.

So it was with great excitement that I read the letter in *Dear Annie* from a woman who wanted information on 'posture bras'. Not only do these wonderful things support you up front, they also pull your shoulders into line. Perfect.

Whether you, too, need help to stand like a supermodel, or are desperate to remove candle wax from a favourite skirt or are pehaps desperate for a specialist dry-cleaner to take care of your precious designer bag, then *Dear Annie*, based on Annalisa Barbieri's fabulously witty and informative column in the *Independent on Sunday*, is the guide for you.

This is a special *Elle* edition. In it are more than 100 of the most-asked fashion questions. All the answers are based on a painstaking amount of research and have been updated to be accurate at time of printing.

I hope you enjoy it and find it as useful as all of us at *Elle*.

Rachel Loos
Acting Editor
Elle

contents

acknowledgements

Since the first 'Dear Annie' appeared in the
Independent on Sunday in 1995, several people have
nurtured the column. But even before its debut, there
were those who gave me guidance and those I assisted;
and with each of them I gathered a little bit more
knowledge and learned a little bit more about fashion.
It is therefore very important that those in the chain of
events bringing me to this book are thanked:

Winston G. Dixon, my very first boss at the Home
Office, who taught me nothing about fashion (other
than that he liked see-through socks), but lots about
office politics. Beverley Cable, for giving me that first
foot in the fashion door, over a decade ago now.
Simon Kelner, my first ever editor (at the *Observer*,
now again my editor at *The Independent*), who gave
me my own page to nurture. Iain R. Webb, who
taught me how to become even more efficient and
organized when I worked with him at *The Times*.
Lowri Turner for giving me so many articles to write
when she was at the *Evening Standard*. Richard
Askwith, perhaps the best copy-editor in the Western
world and then editor of the 'Sunday Review', for asking me to come to the *Independent on Sunday* in the

first place. To Liz Jobey, whom I worked with for only a few months but whose expert journalistic guidance I shall not forget. Jo Dale, for suggesting me to Sue Matthias, my editor on 'Real Life' for over two years, whom I'd also like to thank, hugely, for the chances she has given me and for letting me get on with it. Becky Gardiner, who nurtured and encouraged me in the early days. Clare Mackie, for always being a delight to deal with and for her sublime illustrations on my newspaper columns. To my colleagues for understanding Annie's made-up words and not trying to change them. Thank you to Jan Dalley and Suzi Feay for their book guidance; and to Peter Wilby and Rosie Boycott for all their support. A really big thank you to Jenny Turner for raving about me at dinner with a certain man called Giulio. To dearest Zoe Brown, who has had to put up with ceaseless banter and chatter and then stony book-writing silence, never once getting offended – and for helping to update the 'men and boys' chapter, her specialist subject. Thanks to Rebecca Abbott for helping me update this special *Elle* edition. To John and Lea Hoerner, for the chance to put Dear Annie on-line (www.dearannie.com). And lastly but still most importantly, thank you to my beloved Pete.

introduction

I'm not exactly sure when I first thought of doing a
fashion problem column called 'Dear Annie'. I used to
read the excellent 'Cher Albert' column in the
Evening Standard's *ES* magazine, when Albert Roux
would answer cooking problems in his charming,
quirky way. Sometimes he would be extraordinarily
helpful and at other times (a particularly memorable
occasion was when some fellow asked his opinion of
the microwave) he would be – gently – dismissive. But
he was always very readable.

There was no fashion equivalent to Roux's fabulous
little column. A couple of glossy magazines had questions and answers, but the questions were obviously
made up to fit in with some recently launched product
or shop opening and the answer to everything seemed
to be to go to Manolo Blahnik's and buy a nice pair of
shoes. The fact that not everyone could afford a pair of
Blahnik's wonderful shoes, or lived near his shop in
London, didn't seem to matter. These shallow
columns were token 'help the people' questions and in
reality were anything but. They were, I felt, aimed
more at the industry than at the reader, and that laziness annoyed me.

What I wanted to do was write a column like (I fancied) they had in the forties and fifties, a column with a gentle authority that would answer genuine questions (and yes, all the letters in 'Dear Annie' are genuine) from real people, all over the UK (and the world on some occasions). And wherever possible, the answer would be tailored to their budget and where they lived. 'Dear Annie' is not a lazy column, because real problems are difficult. Real people can't all wear the latest Gucci trousers: they may be too short or too tall, too fat or too broke; they may not live anywhere near a Gucci shop. I knew it wouldn't be easy or particularly glamorous, but I never dreamed it would be so much bloody fun either.

When the 'Real Life' section of the *Independent on Sunday* was first being talked about, back in the spring of 1995, it seemed to be the ideal place to have such a column. Sue Matthias, then editor of 'Real Life', went for the idea immediately and on 13 August 1995 'Dear Annie' appeared for the first time. The questions answered then were all genuine but from friends and colleagues. There was no way for the general public to know about it, yet. For the next few weeks the problems continued to be provided by people I knew; at one point, I wondered if indeed there would ever be any 'real' questions. Maybe people didn't need 'Annie'. (The name comes from the one person in the world who is allowed to call me Annie, a family friend called Pam, whose catchphrase when I was a teenager was 'Oh, *no*, Annie!')

But slowly the letters started to trickle in, and

today the 'Dear Annie' column receives about 150 letters and e-mails a week. (When the column got an e-mail address in early 1997, the amount of men who wrote in shot up so that now there is about an even mix.) Letters from young ladies asking how to wear the latest skirt length, old ladies writing in about their slippers, teenagers asking about skatewear and what to do about their mum's old coat, men wondering where to buy *their* wedding outfits, and lots and lots of letters about bras. The youngest readers to write in have been eight years old, the oldest about ninety and the cross-section is huge. Some letters are funny, some – from post-mastectomy women especially – very sad, but all are lovely to read. Over the three years that Annie has now been going, regular correspondence has built up with some readers: David of London, Mathew from Wales, Vicky from Prague, JL from California, Natalie from London. Despite the 'personal correspondence will not be entered into' rider at the end of the column, I quite often do.

Writing under a pseudonym of sorts is incredibly liberating. Once the research is done, 'Dear Annie' is ludicrously easy to write because it is the real me. And yet, bizarrely, Annie has a life of her own. The moment I sit down, each week, to write the column, I get into character; indeed, I think of Annie as another person altogether, which is why I often refer to her in the third person.

As the letters poured in, it became obvious that there were certain problems that affected lots of people. The first was that people with bigger than average-sized feet found it really difficult to find shoes that fitted properly, let alone that were fashionable. So, in the column on Sunday, I asked for people to write in if they had 'big' feet and knew of any useful contacts, and I also asked for shops and manufacturers to get in touch if they made shoes in sizes bigger than the norm. Most other problem pages provide leaflets covering oft-asked questions ('Send in for my fact sheet on impotence'), so I thought it would be a good idea if Annie also had these. Thus the first directory was born – a nationwide list of useful contacts called the 'Big Shoe' directory. Others followed: 'Size 16 Plus', 'Dressmakers', etc. They were a phenomenal success and we got hundreds of requests a week for copies – these were often sent out late at night when my saner colleagues had gone home.

When I first asked people to send in an SAE (the only payment then required) for the 'Big Shoe' directory, I had vastly underestimated the response and was inundated. With a full-time job on the paper to attend to as well, I fell badly behind. Demand became such that I had to stop sending the directories out. They are now available to read exclusively on my website: www.dearannie.com.

By now, the column had created a little world of its own. At times I would be nervous of not knowing the answer to a question, and often the illustrations for the column would be commissioned *before* I knew if I could even answer the question. But this also proved useful, because it showed that Annie was, ahem, human. It also gave readers the chance to write

in and help – something they do most generously
with 'I know, I know!' letters that put me, and the
original correspondent, out of our misery. The best
and most touching example of this was when Dr
Scott Samuel (see the 'Men and Boys' chapter) asked
for help in finding a pair of old-fashioned black plim-
solls in a size 11 or 12. When another reader wrote in
saying that you could get them in Zimbabwe for a
few pounds, I jokingly said that if anyone went,
could they get Dr Scott Samuel a pair. And someone
did; they went to Zimbabwe and remembered his size
and everything.

In June 1999 Dear Annie went truly global with
the launch of www.dearannie.com. It is updated
every 48 hours with the help of the very diligent
Steve Brown, who is always a joy to work with. The
website was also the obvious place to hold the directories. At the time of writing, two new directories are
being prepared (with a couple more being thought
of). These are the Long Legs Directory and Dry
Cleaners. The first was in response to the many letters I had started getting from readers whose 34" plus
legs they were having difficulty clothing stylishly.
The second will hopefully be a small but nationwide
directory of good dry cleaners, as nominated by
readers. By the time you read this they should be up
and running, if not check back on the website every
now and again.

Annie doesn't care what size people are; all she
cares about is that everyone – be they skinny (yes,
they have just as much right to exist, too), plump,

trendy or not – has the *choice*, the best choice, to wear what they want. She thinks people shouldn't worry too much about clothes. And her greatest weapon is that she doesn't give a hoot about the industry, she doesn't care what's in, she doesn't pander to a particular designer just because he's advertised in the newspaper, she rarely goes to shows and if she does she doesn't care if she's seated in the front row or not.

This book, then, is a compilation of letters printed in the column over the past few years. The very topical questions, about the latest fashions, etc., couldn't be included, because they wouldn't be relevant by the time this book came out and that would just be frustrating for the reader. 'Johnny Loulou' means John Lewis (even some of its staff now refer to this magnificent department store as Johnny Loulou). All the information printed – every phone number, address, name, colour and style – has been checked, updated and revised, but even so it can only be correct at the time of going to press.

breasts
and how best to present them,
plus other useful information for the female form
bras, corsets, girdles and tricks to stop
your bra strap showing

I bought ever such a sweet dress the other day from Top Shop. It has a high neck and cut-away arms. But I just cannot find a bra with straps that don't show and I don't want to go without.
– *Barbara Evans, Abergavenny*

How wise of you not to leave your bosoms to gravity. You could wear a sports bra – the ones with racing backs would be perfect, as the front straps are also set in more than on conventional bras. But if you want to wear something prettier, or if you don't want to disrobe to reveal a rather unsexy sporting model, then wear your favourite, sexiest, blackest bra or body and tie a thin piece of elastic or ribbon to pull together (but not join) the two front (yes, front not back) straps. You'll have to experiment to see exactly what length of elastic/ribbon is best for you. This is good for two reasons: first, if a bit of bra does show, it's better that it's of the coronary-inducing variety. And, second, tying elastic/ribbon in this way pushes your quarter-pounders together to give you a cor-blimey silhouette. Elastic works best as it provides 'give' as you move (discreetly retire to the bathroom and cut it off before you undress), but if you plan to disrobe – or be disrobed – fast, then ribbon is recommended.

I followed your advice on how to wear a bra under a cut-out-arm dress and it worked brilliantly. I have a different problem: I have a great black Tactel short slip dress with shoestring straps from Marks & Spencer but I have to wear a bra (I'm a 36C). This means I can never wear it without something over the top. I think strapless bras look terrible on me – they give me a sausage-type chest – and I cannot afford to go to a fancy lingerie shop and have a bra made for me. Can I ever wear this dress and reveal my shoulders? – *Desperate, Dulwich*

Yes, it's great having bosoms but don't you wish you could get rid of them when you want to wear slip dresses with spaghetti straps? Don't you get sick of having to wear cute little T-shirts under the dress to hide the bra straps, or being forced to wear a bloody cardie? This trick takes only a little bit of time, but it works and can hopefully be used with a bra you already have. What you do is sew together the back straps of the dress, just for about an inch so that they come together at about the middle of your shoulder blades. This will make the neckline a bit higher, but will not make any difference to the dress you have. Then basically you do the same to the bra. Lengthen the straps so they're so long that the metal 'buckle' bit is hidden by the dress at the back. Then sew it together at the back so that it matches up to the dress. You need a bra with simple flat straps (none of those fancy ruched numbers for this) and you can sew it and then slip it over your head (the same goes for the dress). It lifts your breasts up a treat and from the back it looks like you have on a multi-strapped dress. When you're done, you just unpick the stitches. Like my other bra trick, you can't undress in a hurry or when drunk, but who cares?

I have an older sister who is a completely different shape to me, she is flat-chested and I have a large bust. We still live at home and argue endlessly about sharing clothes. She won't let me near any of hers, saying I misshape them. The latest row was over her polo-neck jumper – she says it doesn't suit me as it makes my bust look bigger. I hate my bust anyway, but do you think she is right?
– *Depressed, Middlesex*

It depends. A *baggy* polo-neck jumper – like any baggy jumper – is not the most flattering thing to wear if you have a large bust, as it falls from your chest to make you look bigger than you are. But a tight jumper with a well-fitting bra (go for something like Playtex's Cross Your Heart bra for torpedo-shaped breasts) will look fantastic. Let your sister have her moment of glory; there has been so much press of late on how attractive big bosoms are, she may well be feeling jealous. V-neck jumpers are anyhow far more flattering to a larger bust, so leave her with hers and hunt out one of your own.

You seem very good on bra-related questions. I have a size 34D bust and want to wear a Wonderbra, but they only go up to a cup size C. Just because I have a D-cup bosom doesn't mean I don't also want to wear a Wonderbra. – *D. Collins, Derby*

Being a bit greedy, aren't you? Only joking. Well, the good news is that Wonderbra *do* go up to a D-cup in their 'main' range and in some of the specials they do, but some – like the current Smashing Venus range – only go up to C-cup. Or you may want to follow the advice of the American writer (and bosom and flirt expert) Dianne Brill and get a cup size smaller and a chest size bigger than you would normally wear (i.e., in your case a 36C). Hasn't done her any harm. Bravissimo (020 8742 8882, www.bravissimo.com) do four 'plunge' bras (which is afterall, what a Wonderbra is) from Warners, Triumph, Gossard and Panache. Three of these start at a D-cup (the other one starts at DD). For others interested they go up to F (G on one model). Prices from £25.30, colours: mainly black and white. And the wonderful Margaret Ann could order one from the mega-sexy Goddess range from America, so call her on 01985 840520. And yes, if I had £1 for every question I was asked about bosoms, I'd be really rich, so if anyone has a bra-related problem, please send £1 in with your query.

Where can I buy a corset for that 'nipped-in waist' look? The only ones I have seen are either silly prices or advertised by dubious 'specialist' shops. – Katie Wilson (Miss), Leicester
OK, Vollers, the corset company in Portsmouth, make very traditional corsets (all their patterns are 100 years old) which cost between £80 and £350, from sizes 18" (sharp intake of breath) to 38" (aaaaah), and there is a made-to-measure service. Call them on 01705 799030. They also do a catalogue. Bellers of Islington, 193 Upper Street London N1 1RQ, tel: 020 7226 2322, do a full range of corsetry. The more old-fashioned laced-back stuff is available in sizes 26" to 44" waist, and the more modern stuff, which was described as 'Pride and Prejudice', comes in sizes 10 to 18, all from about £50.

Margaret Ann (01985 840520) can offer all sorts of
boned stuff, including an own-label range, from £80.
And finally Axfords (01273 327944, www.axfords.com,
e-mail: axfords@axfords.com) make some lovely, reasonably priced corsets from £60 for a waist-cincher to £230
for a leather corset. There is a rather saucy catalogue
available which costs £10.

**I've read that toupee tape is good for use as a bra in very
compromising dresses and I'm keen to try it (does it work?).
But where oh where do I buy it?** – *Helena, Bridport*
I've heard fairly good reports about this although I've
never been able to try it since my bosoms, as so often
reported, need a little bit more support than can be
provided by toupee tape. Anywhere that sells wigs
sells it. I say this even though I know it sounds obvious but wiggy shops are places we tend not to see
unless we suddenly need a wig. The nearest place I
could find to you according to the local Yellow Pages
is the Dorset Wig Co., 5 Post Office Road,
Bournemouth, Dorset, tel: 01202 291887. But they
have yet to return my calls. Never mind because
Trendco (01273 774977) sell toupee tape, altough they
call it Monotape. It is five metres long and 1" wide and
costs £3.99 plus £1.25 for p&p. It is also hypoaller-
genic which is useful as improvising with parcel tape
as one of my friends did in her teenage youth gave her
a nasty rash.

**I have always had very bad posture and as I am getting older
the problem is getting worse. (To the extent that if I don't
find a solution soon, I will be staring my navel in the eye!) A**

friend once told me about 'posture bras'. Have you heard of
such a thing? Can you suggest any other solution?
– *Liela Hekmatyar, York*

Yes, I have. A posture back bra does up at the front
and has a full back, usually with criss-cross panels. It
helps correct posture by supporting the upper back
and encouraging you to keep your shoulders straight.
Exquisite Form does one style in its Fully range. Style
531 comes in white and costs £18. It is available in
sizes 34–44B/34–46/C 34–46D and 36–46DD. There is a
freephone consumer advice line (0800 592553) which
will put you in touch with stockists. It is also worth
working on your latissimus dorsi (the muscles under
the shoulders), as this will help take the strain off a
larger bust (if that is your problem) and aid posture.

I have bought my girlfriend a slinky, strappy, backless dress.
She is large- breasted, so must wear a bra, but all the ones
she has show. I seem to remember that you've already given
advice about this problem in your column – could you send me
copies of your answers. – *Derek O'Carroll, Glasgow*

The advice I have given before was for wearing a bra
with a dress with cut-out shoulders, or a strappy dress
with a not-so-low back. With a backless *and* strappy
dress, things are a little more difficult. Really, I do
think you could have given a little more thought to
your girlfriend's natural shape when making this
otherwise generous offer. There is little alternative
than for her to wear a basque with a very low back.
Rigby and Peller in London (020 7589 9293) do some
fabulous ones from about £50. They provide a mail

order seven-day approval service (although of course nothing beats a personal fitting) so your girlfriend can phone up, tell them what she's looking for and what size she is. She can then give them *your* credit card details as security and they can send stuff out on approval. If the items don't suit she can return them and as long as they are in perfect condition your credit card will be refunded.

I think there is something wrong with me. I wear cleavage bras but somehow my breasts don't seem to 'meet', if you see what I mean. It's almost like the cups should be closer together. Do you have any ideas? – Michaela Walker, St Ives
First, with bras such as these you have to wear them slightly differently. Adjust the straps so that they are shorter than you would normally wear them. Then stuff the sides (i.e., like where the outside of your breast is, and underneath so you prop them up and in) with something like old tights. This doesn't sound very attractive but if you cut up a pair of old tights (preferably in the same colour as your bra) these are ideal for 'stuffing' as the fabric is pliable. Some bras also come with foam fillers, which are useful but never big enough. Make sure whatever you stuff your bra with isn't too 'solid' (which is why tights are so good) because not only is this uncomfortable but it will also give you a lumpy silhouette, and we don't want that.

Can you advise me on how to dress to disguise the fact that my breasts are different sizes? Underwear isn't a problem as I wear a soft bra (I'm very small anyway), so it doesn't matter that one side is slightly too big. With a leotard I wear some-

thing loose on top, and when I go swimming I grit my teeth
and scuttle between changing room and pool as fast as possible. Ordinary clothes are the problem. I can never wear
anything that fits; I live in very loose things. I've heard that
patterned fabric is best for this kind of thing, but I tried
something on in a shop this morning with narrow horizontal
stripes and it just seemed to accentuate the difference in
size, and really upset me – I looked horrible. I don't know
how obvious it is to other people but to me it's the most
noticeable thing about me. Can you give me any tips?
– *Jane Gibson, West Yorkshire*

I guess you're hoping that I can provide some miracle
solution. I can't. I do so understand what it is like to
try something on and feel that you look awful. This is
why I rarely buy clothes – I can't bear to try them on
in shops as my mood for the rest of the day is reliant
on what I'll look like. The mistake you made, I think,
is that stripes most probably will make things worse.
Stripes can act like a grid system, accentuating all the
wrong bits; by which I mean the bits *you* don't like.
How different in size could your breasts be? Not
much. The problem is in your head, and while I realize
that this still makes it a problem (hence when we feel
fat and ugly no matter what people say to make us feel
better, we still feel fat and ugly), it is a problem that
cannot be helped by any tips I can give you. Yes, patterned (abstract, floral, etc.) fabrics do 'fuzz' silhou-
ettes and take the focus away from your shape and on
to the pattern. You could also, I guess, pad one cup
out slightly to make it look like the bigger breast. But
there is *no reason at all* to skulk around wearing loose

tops or to jettison yourself from changing room to swimming pool. The only thing that will effectively disguise your shape is to carry on wearing loose clothes, but do you really want to do this? What a waste. Unless you are a freak, in which case I would already have read about you in the *Sunday Sport*, any difference in the size of your breasts will be imperceptible. It is completely natural for one bosom to be slightly bigger than the other, usually the side that is more well developed (i.e., if you are right-handed the right-hand side of your body will usually be slightly larger). I am sorry if you were hoping for names and addresses of companies that do clothes to disguise this problem but I cannot advise you to hide something that is completely natural.

I bought the Marks & Spencer black Tactel slip that you've mentioned a few times. It is wonderful. However, as you know, it has shoestring straps and I cannot wear it without a bra. I've tried strapless ones, etc., but my bust is quite large (34DD) and believe me it does not look good with a strapless bra. It looks great with a bra underneath but obviously you can see it (the straps don't match up, one comes in more than the other). I thought if anyone could help, you could. Please do! – *Georgia, Plymouth*

OK, you have come to the right place. Thank you for your drawing to show me what the problem is, but it is easily solved. I know exactly what you mean. First, you have to get a black bra whose strap is as simple as possible – no fancy lace, scalloping or beefy belt-size straps. Then put on the bra, put the dress on top and

move the dress around by pulling it slightly under the
arms (effectively stretching it out a bit) until the straps
are one on top of the other, then just run a few stitches
along (sort of under the arm) to join the dress to the
bra. Tactel is a wonder fibre, although it is just good
old nylon, which is the generic name for Tactel, and
the dress will easily get back into shape. It will look
like your dress straps and your bra straps are one. I
find people are always afraid to 'stitch themselves' into
clothing, but it is not frightening. Often a quick one,
two with a needle and thread can make all the difference and remove the need for fidgeting.

**I enjoy wearing T-shirts, but as I get older my boobs shrink and
my nipples seem to stick out more and are visible under some
tops. Can you recommend a bra with smooth lines (no seams)
but thick enough to mask the nipple? – *Henrietta, Devon***
The other day at a friend's party, I noticed that my
friend Alex's bosoms looked incredibly pert under a
chiffon top. So I said, 'Alex, your breasts look incredibly perky. What's up?' It transpired that she had two
Gossard Glossies sheer bras on, because, she said, it
stopped her nipps showing. It worked, but you might
find this a) extreme and b) expensive. What she didn't
know is that Gossard Glossies do an opaque bra
(£19.00 for the underwired bra, different shades available) which stops you having nipple show-through
and is seamless. They are available in loads of places;
call 01525 859769. Warners also do a great range called
'Simply Smooth' which is fantastic for nipple show-
through. Three styles of bra range from 32–42 AA–FF

(but not in all styles), £23 and in black, white and nude. Call 0115 9795796 for stockists near you.

I had a baby by Caesarean six months ago and have seen my skirt size go from 12 to 16. I have a number of outfits which still fit my top half, but not at the bottom. I don't like exercise or dieting, so a friend suggested a panty girdle or control-top tights. I have tried control briefs and they are some help. I don't mind a bit of discomfort in the pursuit of fashion and have had a look at a girdle, but am not sure which one is best to flatter my tummy. Can you make any suggestions? (Playtex '18 hour'?) – *J. Morgan*

You didn't put an address so I have no idea where you are. Yes, well, who does like exercise or dieting, eh? But I have to say that sit-ups do help, and one can do these while watching telly, or even eating crisps, or even smoking (*Smoke and Stretch*, my new video, out soon). I do think a girdle would be best for you. I hate them, as I feel constricted in them, but if you don't mind a bit of discomfort then these will give the best results. Good old Playtex of those famous 18-hour-promise ads do have a good selection of panty girdles with high waists or lower waists. They really strap you in and provide firm control on the tummy. Prices start at £22.50 and range up to £35; call 0500 362430 for your nearest stockist (Johnny Loulou have the 18-hour waist girdle [style no. 2697], £25.50, and the 18-hour panty girdle [style no. 2690], £27.50, available from selected branches; enquiries 020 7629 7711). Playtex also do a 'Body Solutions' range called Superlook Secrets, which controls hips, bottom, stomach, etc.

Prices start at £10 per brief (sizes 10–22) and £18 for
bras (34"–38" BCD). And Marks & Spencer also have a
wide selection of fabulous control underwear, from
thigh slimmers and waist slimmers (which claim to take
2" off the waist!) to tummy slimmers. Prices start at
£10.00 from branches nationwide (020 7935 4422).
Damart also have a selection of pantie girdles from
£7.99 (which my mum swears by, she won't have any
others). To order a catalogue call 01274 510000.
Control-top tights are OK (and just about everyone
does a pair, though I've yet to find one brand radically
better than another), but they won't really hold you in
in the way you seem to want.

pane, amore e cha cha cha
this means 'bread, love and chitter-chatter'
in italian and this chapter is all about crafty
and useful tips, mostly learned in italy
*how to clean suede, get wax out of clothes
and chewing gum out of hair*

I wear a lot of black and am forever getting fluff on my clothes which looks awful. None of those brushes advertised as defluffers works. Is there any way to look well groomed? – C. Forbes (Ms), Bristol

You can get those contraptions that roll around and have replaceable sheets of stickiness, or those ones that are meant to 'reactivate' under the auspices of a good run under a cold tap. To my mind, they are all crap. The best, cheapest and only way to defluff is to get some good old parcel tape (sticky tape will do too, but parcel tape tends to be more adhesive and covers more square inches at a time). Take a length of tape and stick it round your hand and then just work your way over the garment. Easy-peasy and bloody cheap.

I have this wonderful cotton coat that I bought years ago. It's black cotton jersey and I wear it with everything. The problem is that I went to a dinner party and the hostess put my coat on a chair that was underneath a candle and now I have candle wax all over it. I've tried picking it off but it doesn't work. Should I wash it? – *Sue Paige, Southampton*

Sue the bloody stupid hostess. Damn nuisance. Nah, don't bother picking it off and don't wash it. What

you do is put some brown paper over it and iron it.
The wax will melt and be absorbed by the brown
paper and will disappear from your beloved coat.
Make sure the iron is clean (when it's cool) before you
use it again and next time make sure the dippy hostess
trying to re-create a scene from *Dracula* has a proper
place to hang your coat. Damn nuisance.

I have a long white satin skirt that I love wearing but it is a
bit see-through. I hate wearing G-strings and none of the
skin-tone knickers I have tried seems 'thin' enough (you can
still see the line of the knickers). Surely someone somewhere has done a gossamer-thin pair of briefs?
– *Franca Malson, Bedford*
If you really feel that the range of skin-tone knickers
that is currently on the market is not suitable (and
M&S do an excellent selection), then try this: take two
pairs of fine-denier tights, chop them off at mid-thigh
and wear them instead of underwear. This is not recommended for everyday use (nylon next to your cha
cha is not the healthiest thing) but it is an excellent
solution to your problem and one used by stylists
caught out on fashion shoots. Very unattractive to
look at, so avoid high gales.

I am always getting make-up on my clothes as I pull the garment over my head. I can't always get dressed before apply-
ing make-up. What do you do? – *Emma Phillips,
Barrow-in-Furness*
This isn't a problem I have as I have never managed to
work out the difference between an eye pencil and a lip
pencil. I even eat off my lip gloss, when I think to apply

it. Sadly, between bringing up babies and running a pig farm, make-up has got lost along the way. But this is what models do on shoots, when make-up is always applied before dressing. Buy some synthetic georgette from your local department store, about half a metre. Then, put it over your head before you slip your clothes on. The georgette will protect your clothes but still allow you to get dressed easily (and still allow you to see – always handy to prevent claustrophobia attacks). If you're not too drunk when you get home, remember to do it when you get undressed too (although in reverse the process is more fiddly). Works like magic.

I like to wear shirts outside my trousers but find that when I wear a jacket on the way to work the shirt tails are always longer than the jacket. Should I make a feature of this or wear longer jackets? – *M. Donaghy (Mrs), Bath*

If you want to make a feature of the shirt tails you could also pull the shirt cuffs so that they peek out of the jacket sleeves and all this spillage looks intentional rather than just scruffy. You could buy a longer-length jacket, but if your shirt tails are that long, to cover them you will end up with a very long jacket and looking like a Teddy boy. Is shortening the shirt not an option? But perhaps the simplest way is to get a length of thick, soft elastic, tying it into a circle, stepping into it so that it sits over your shirt and then pulling the shirt up until its hem sits comfortably above your jacket hem. When you reach your destination pull the shirt tails out of the elastic which remains discreetly about your waist awaiting the journey home.

What is the best way to get chewing gum out of clothes?
– Arantxa, Sutton Coldfield

You need to freeze the garment, then the gum will just
snap off. Incidentally, if anyone ever gets chewing
gum in their hair, a very nice man at Wrigley's told me
the trick is either to get some cocoa butter (from
chemists) and work it into the hair and then wash as
normal (it dissolves the chewing gum), or, if you can't
get hold of that, mix fat or butter with chocolate or
cocoa powder (if necessary heat it up and then let it
cool until it is still malleable but not hot) and then
work the paste into the hair and wash. Rather handy
trick, I thought. Thank you, Wrigley's.

**Could you please give me some advice on caring for buck
leather? I recently bought a pair of black ankle boots which I
sprayed with matt leather dressing before I wore them, but
now, after several wearings, they have become a little
marked and I should like to know the best way to keep them
clean. – Val Bardsley (Mrs), Norwich**

Buck, or nubuck, leather needs special care as it is
more delicate and finer than conventional leather and
suedes. You could try Meltonian's Suede and Nubuck
Cleaning Block (£2.85), enquiries: 01753 523 971. It
removes mild spots and stains and is suitable for any
colour. When suede and nubuck become worn they
are susceptible to shiny bald patches, just like tired old
men, and this block restores texture (to shoes, not
heads). What I do, though, is rub my nubuck and
suede shoes very lightly with a fine sandpaper. On
light-coloured suede/nubuck, I dust them with talc

and then brush it off with a soft brush (I find babies'
toothbrushes are ideal for this). If they're quite dirty, I
hold the shoe over a steaming kettle and gently brush
the pile with this soft brush; the steam cleans the
suede/nubuck. On black suede or nubuck, nothing
beats holding the shoe over a candle and brushing gently. This is what my mother used to do with all her
fine suede stilettos as a youngster; the soot kind of
rejuvenates black suede.

stockings and suspenders
plus boring stuff too about tights and socks
*where to get a six-strap suspender belt,
silk socks and airy tights*

I enjoy wearing fully fashioned seamed stockings with suspenders for their feel and glamorous looks. However, it is difficult to keep the seams straight over a long period and there is nothing worse than crooked seams for ruining the glamorous effect. Do you have any useful advice? A suspender belt with six straps might help but does anyone manufacture such a thing? – G. Roper (Mrs), Peterborough, Cambs

Yes, I do know someone who makes a six-strap suspender thing and that will help keep your seams straight, but just before I launch into that let me say that what will also help is if you wear a 'deep' suspender belt, i.e., one that has a substantial piece of material to it that really anchors the s/b to your hips and not one that is just a flimsy strip of material. Now then, try Cover Girl Shoes, 5 Packington Workshops, 10 Packington Square, London N1, tel: 020 7354 2883. This is ostensibly a shop for transvestites but they are very helpful and sell six-strap suspender belts with metal clasps for about £30.

I have a very annoying problem. *All* my tights give at the seams, even at the first wear! I am 5'5", with my widest point (at the top of my thighs) approx. 41". I weigh just under ten

stone and normally wear size 14 skirts. I have tried nail varnish on a new tear but it makes it worse. What would you suggest?
– *Helen, London*

I am not sure what you mean by 'they give at the seams' as most tights do not have seams other than around the top. Is this where they give? First, look for tights with Lycra in them. This fibre has 'stretch and recover' properties and for hosiery manufacturers to be able to include Lycra in their product, DuPont (Lycra's manufacturers) insist that the tights meet various criteria – such as having a gusset. A gusset on tights ensures that you can walk without pulling on the seams too much. You are not fat, so that is not causing the problem (in any case, tights, like condoms, are miraculous things that stretch beyond all imagination). Having said that, are you sure you are buying tights that are big enough for you? I always find that people buy tights too small for them, somehow thinking that 'large' is for people who are six foot tall. I never buy smaller than a medium, even though according to the packet size-guide I should be buying small. But getting them in a size bigger means you don't have to pull on them so much. Nail varnish should work – you need to apply it to the bottom and top of a new tear, although this is only a temporary measure. I wear mostly Wolford as I think their quality is superb, especially their opaques, some of which I've had for years. You might also like to pop down to Fogal, in London, with stores in Sloane Street and New Bond Street. They make very expensive and very good hosiery and are also most knowledgeable.

I've been trying to get hold of a pair of black over-the-knee socks but to no avail. I am desperate to get hold of a pair as I have got quite nice legs and they will look very sexy with my miniskirt. I know they were all the rage about twelve months ago but no one seems to sell them/wear them any more. Please help – *Julia, Salisbury*

Johnny Loulou still do them, two types: a wool/Lycra mix (called Jonelle) for £3.45 and a cotton mix called the KS, £3.95 (enquiries: 020 7629 7711).

Your advice about shoulder pads and see-through blouses inspired me to write in [see 'Can I, Should I?' chapter]. Do you also consider it tacky for me to show the 'bumps' of my suspenders when wearing a straight skirt? I don't wear skin-tight skirts and always ensure that I wear a slip or that they are lined. A short time ago, when suspenders were very much in fashion, we all couldn't help showing our bumps, but now that stockings aren't so widely worn I feel rather out on a limb. So what do you think, am I the strumpet that some of my friends say I am? – *Shelly, Wilmslow*

The wearing of suspenders does not *make* you a strumpet, Shelly. This involves other things, such as the frequent and sometimes inappropriate removal of one's pants in the company of surname-not-known gentlemen. *Au fait* I predict that – with the onward march of Miuccia Prada's feminine dressing – suspenders will be much more widely worn this winter. A hint of suspender is rather nice, I think. I know what you mean, though. I love wearing stockings and suspenders, but only dare do so with a particular skirt that is long, lined and of fairly thick

crêpe. Then it is only obvious that I am wearing
them when I sit on my husband's lap (or anyone
else's, if I am very drunk). I should continue with
your sensible use of them – and your friends are
obviously jealous, because we all know that stockings and suspenders are by far the sexiest form of
hosiery, it's just that most of us can't be figged to
wear them.

I have always followed Marlene Dietrich's advice (does any
girl today know who that glamour queen was?) to wear
shoes as close as possible to the skin tone of the leg, for a
longer, slimmer silhouette. It lifts short girls and slims
plump girls and is easy on the purse because the 'long
naked leg' illusion matches red, blue, green and even black.
– *Magda, Gibraltar*

Thanks, Magda, for your words of Gibraltarian wis-
dom, although I disagree with you on the source of this
advice – I think it was Marilyn Monroe. You are right,
though, that wearing skin-tone shoes does indeed make
your legs look longer (obviously you need to wear
skin-tone hosiery, too, if you cannot go bare-legged),
but they aren't quite as versatile as you make out. If
your skin tone is of the pinky-beige variety, then wearing matching shoes will not really go with dark suits; I
think it looks naff and odd. It is ideal, however, for
summer wear or if you are wearing an outfit of a difficult colour (i.e., turquoise or yellow), as buying matching shoes for such a garment would be difficult.

I am a size 16–18 and have difficulty finding stockings that fit
well. All of the stockings that I have tried run short, and the

tops finish halfway up my thigh, making them difficult to secure to suspenders. I have tried a variety of brands in their 'Large' size without success. Can you please help? Thanks and regards. – *Jackie, Kent*

Independence Ltd (01353 667722 for mail order) have extra-long stockings in 20 and 30 denier in honey or mink, £6.50 for three pairs, £10.99 for six pairs.

And Magnus (tel: 01604 831271), who also make shoes in larger sizes [see 'Big Shoe' directory on www.dearannie.com] also sell extra-long stockings and tights which fit up to a size 22. Evans do both stockings and tights in their branches nationwide (enquiries: 020 7291 2405). Stockings come in natural or black, £3.50, and are one size. In tights there is a good selection, including glossies, run-resistant, sheer and opaques in winter. They start at £3.50 and they begin at 12 denier, in three sizes: 48", 52" and 60" hips. [Also make sure you read my advice about six-strap suspenders earlier in this chapter.] Also try Margaret Ann (01985 8405207).

Please help! I used to buy tights with a gusset gap ('airflow tights') which let the body breathe, so there was no odour. I got these from Tytex/Better Living mail order, but they seem to have closed down or moved. Can I get such tights any-where? If your information scouts could come up with a source I'd be very grateful. – *Sarah V., Athens*

Well, your letter came on hotel paper from a five-star hotel in Athens (fancy), so I can only assume you actually live in the UK. (I am flattered that on holiday you thought to write to me . . .) One tip is to cut the diamond gusset shape carefully out of a 'normal' pair of tights to allow for extra ventilation, or you could try Bhs's Body-Free tights, £5 for two (enquiries: 020 7262 3288). And Priory Healthcare do some (from £6.45 for four pairs + p&p; 01438 798 206), as do Aldrex (from £6.99 for three; write to Aldrex, Dept ALD 1021, Brandlesholme Road, Bury BL8 1BG or call 0161 236 5555 for a catalogue). Finally, try Woman in Mind (01204 525 115, mail order only), who make all sorts of hosiery (Ventights, Open Crotch Tights) and whose priority is making sure there is a supply of fresh air to your cha cha.

can i? should i?
sometimes
reassurance for the confused: how to wear things, when to wear them . . . sartorial correctness if such a thing exists

I am going to a wedding in August (who isn't?) and wearing a hat for the first time ever! Does one keep one's hat on during the meal? I presume I shall have to discard it by the time I get to the dance floor. I wouldn't normally bother busy people like you with my limited knowledge of fashion protocol, but I can't find the answer to my question in any etiquette books.
– *Barbara King, Lancashire*

Well, I'm not going to a wedding in August, regrettably, as I always find them a great deal of fun. In matters of fashion protocol, I am not much good, since I believe that as long as you don't offend anyone and carry it off with aplomb you should do what you want. My thoughts, however, are that eating with a hat is rather superfluous, especially if the hat is big. Will your hat be easy to take on and off? By that I mean will taking it off mean a half-hour trip to the ladies' to rearrange your hair? Does your outfit *need* the hat and does the removal of your headgear therefore make your outfit 'too simple'? These are things you need to think about, but not for too long. I don't think I have ever been to a wedding that involved hats, and certainly don't remember any at the table. (My best friend, Lily, once went to a wedding where her Aunt Catherine kept

her hat on and secreted all manner of antipasto under it,
to take home to give to her cats – she was that sort of
woman – but I doubt you will be doing that.) Men
remove their top hats (if they are wearing them) at the
table, and I think it only fair, in the interests of equality,
that women do the same. I would perhaps keep the hat
on when you first sit down, if toasts and whatnot are
performed at the beginning of the meal, and then take it
off for eating. But ultimately, do what feels comfortable
and sod protocol.

Is it OK to wear a G-string with a short skirt?
– Sally Tyvek, Sidcup

There was once a girl of my acquaintance who wore
thong panties constantly. She also had a penchant for
miniskirts, and usually combined the two very well. She
was careful, you know, bending over and climbing up
stairs (maintaining a straight back, she informed me,
was the key to a successful discreet ascent). Then, one
horrible day, she brought a rucksack to work with her
when rucksacks were just becoming fashionable (this
girl was at the cutting edge of fashion). She hitched it on
to her back, not noticing, dear reader, that the rucksack
had hitched up her short skirt with it. She happily
walked to work thinking she must look very good
indeed today: she could hear wolf whistles behind her
and builders swung off scaffolding shouting urgent
things at her. It was only when she got to work and
stood in the mirrored-wall lift that she realized her bottom was on general display. She was never the same
after that. Other than avoiding rucksacks, there is no

reason why you shouldn't wear G-strings under a short
skirt. Personally I can't see why you can't wear anything you want under a short skirt, including nothing at
all if the fancy takes you (provided you are careful, so as
not to get arrested for indecency). And be extra careful
going up escalators. If you see a gaggle of men loitering
at the bottom with a zoom-lens camera, you can bet it's
not the novelty-painted ceiling they're snapping.

**Can you solve a long-running argument? Should knitwear be
folded or hung and if hung, on what sort of hanger?**
– Betsy, London
Knitwear should really be folded because hanging
can stretch it. However this is not always possible and
some knitwear (i.e. lighter things that don't stretch
under their own weight) are fine on a hanger. But it
should be a padded hanger with good, thick padding.
John Lewis (0202 7629 7711) always have some, starting from £4 (although lately their selection has been
awful) and Cath Kidston has done some very pretty
ones for £6 (020 7229 8000).

**Is it OK to wear navy with black? And what about blue with
green? – Veronica Walsh, Lewisham**
Yes, yes.

How high should heels be for work? – Tessa Malcolm, St Ives
What sort of work? Generally, as long as you can walk
in them then they are OK. If you are a prozzie, then I
guess they can be as high as you like as you will spend
most of your time lying down, or against a wall. A
rule of thumb is: if the ball of your foot still touches

the floor, then you're OK. If not, we're talking fetish.

I have a black sleeveless dress. Sometimes my bra (black) strap peeks out from under my dress. I think it looks quite sweet, but my friend recently told me it looks tarty. What do you think? – *Esther Connell-Turner, Taunton*

I agree with you that a bit of bra strap showing can look nice. After all, it is nothing to be ashamed of. In places like Spain and Italy, women frequently have bra straps showing. Far better to be confident with a bit of peek-a-boo strap than to be constantly fiddling to tuck it in. What sort of friend tells you that you look tarty with so little provocation? I'll bet she has washerwoman's upper arms and so never dares to show hers. Next time your friend comments on your bra strap, mention that you have some sheets that need washing.

I like wearing fairly see-through blouses and am careful to wear 'matching' bras: i.e., black for black, cream for cream, etc. Most of these shirts have shoulder pads which you can see. Someone at work said this was highly tacky. Is it? – *Wanda, Shropshire*

I'd say. Although I am mellowing in my old age and think people should essentially wear what they wish to, I can't help thinking that a see-through blouse is the woman's equivalent of a red sports car. And why were you wearing such a thing at work? Anyway, you have asked me one thing and I must stick to the point. Shoulder pads are suspect at the best of times (although they keep trying to make a comeback, thanks mostly to Alexander McQueen), so visible shoulder pads become very suspect things indeed. If you must wear blouses

that show your bra, please take the shoulder pads out.
If necessary, wear them as blinkers.

There is this girl at work who keeps telling me that my skirts
are too short. I am twenty-one, have nice legs (I think) and
wear opaque tights and low shoes with them. I am very careful when I bend down. She says short skirts are very 1980s
and now women don't have to show their legs, but I like
wearing short skirts and don't think I'll be able to wear them
when I'm older. What do you think? – *Simone, Portsmouth*
Oh yes, and what does she look like? Like a sumo
wrestler, I'll bet. Women can be their own worst ene-
my. I can't stand this female bitchy backhandedness.
You sound sensible, sexy and nice. Of course you can
wear short skirts. Women have a choice now and
you've made yours. Next time sumo makes a com-
ment, smile and say, 'Goodness, you look nice today.
Where's that lovely jumper/skirt/tent from?' This'll
fox her. As one of the characters in *Absolutely
Fabulous* once said, 'In with anger, out with love.'

I have one quick question for you. I know you have a huge
waiting list, but please, please try to fit this in. I saw a Jil
Sander suit which is a shade over £1,000 (I can't write the
exact figure in, I'm too embarrassed). I'm not rich but I can
just afford it. I am in a total quandary as to whether to buy it.
I'm usually decisive but I CAN'T DECIDE WHAT TO DO. All my
friends say I am mad to spend so much on a suit. Should I
buy it? – *Rebecca, Kent*
Oh, Rebecca. You want me to give you permission,
don't you? You want me to say, 'It's OK, it's invest-
ment dressing.' Stop getting yourself into such a flap.

Buy the suit. Jil Sander is a supremely classic designer and you will no doubt wear it loads. It will not go out of fashion and as long as you're not going to starve if you spend the money on this suit, then OF COURSE YOU SHOULD BUY IT, YOU SILLY GIRL. Anyway, wearing a Jil Sander suit will no doubt elicit all sorts of dinner-date invites, so you won't go hungry. Your friends are obviously jealous. So start practising writing the amount on your chequebook. P.S. Don't even consider having children if the purchase of an item of clothing reduces you to a gibbering, indecisive wreck.

Is it ever acceptable to wear tights with open-toed sandals? Of course I mean very sheer, natural tights. Are they OK, or does that webbing-effect round the toes look a bit strange?
– Hester, Battersea

No, it's not, and yes, it does. Acknowledge the seasons with your little feet, Hester, and let them go naked when the sun shines.

If I buy a Moschino bikini costing £100, is it all right to wear the knickers inside out so that the label shows?
– A. MacDonald (Mrs), Dorset

Oh dear, no. People will think you have gone quite mad if you wander round the beach with your gusset on show. Surely the stupendous cut of the Moschino bikini will indicate it is a designer number and not something you picked off the floor in some cheap store's changing rooms.

hidey-holes
how to hide the things you don't like and show off those you do
this deals with the serious: from turbans for chemotherapy patients to the everyday problem of how to hide tummies, and also how best to show off nice things like curves

I am thirty years old, 5'7", and my statistics are 36–28–35. My legs are quite long, which means that, as well as being thick-waisted, I am short-bodied. What can I wear to disguise this awful middle of mine, as no amount of exercise seems to help? P.S. I have awful problems with evening wear.
– *Juliette Wills, Devon*

Your middle is not awful in the slightest. The supposed 'ideal' is having bust and hip measurements that are the same and the waist ten inches less that this (i.e., 36, 26, 36), so yours are just a few inches off being bloody perfect, you lucky cow. You also are fairly tall with long legs. You need a good slap round the head, my dear, for there is nothing wrong with you. But anyway, you see this as a problem. What not to wear are things like baggy jumpers, which obviously have their purpose, and I'll bet you've been wearing a fair few of these in order to disguise that middle of yours. Don't. Wear lots of fitted jackets. Get any old cardigans and chop them off to just under bosom level. This defines your waist and makes your body look longer. Belts also highlight the waist (although I can't bear to wear them). Evening wear? Get your legs out, wear shimmering sheer tights and a miniskirt or hot pants (yes, really), fluff your cleavage

up and forget about your waist. Your admirers will find
it for you as they snake their hopeful arms around it.
[God, I feel quite depressed now. I have taken to snatch-
ing chocolate *from my children's hands* as I write this
book. Today I ate a creme egg before I had even entered
one chapter and I am forced to hide wrappers down my
sofa's cleavage.]

I know everyone says this to you all the time, but I really love
your column. I have three problems: I have a large bosom,
very small waist and the biggest bum in the world, honestly.
I look best in little agnes b T-shirts, which make my chest
practically disappear and show off my waist, but then I can't
walk out of a room without putting on a coat to cover my
bum. What should I be wearing? Are hipsters right out?
Why didn't Vivienne Westwood succeed in making bottoms
fashionable? – *Kate, London*

I can't understand how little agnes b T-shirts make
your chest practically disappear but it obviously
works for you, so good. It is pointless me saying 'go
here and buy this', since I don't think this is the sort
of advice you need. There are certain things that
might work for you, and here is a selection. First and
most importantly, being confident about how you
are is *everything*; before you sigh and say 'I know
that', you obviously aren't – yet. When I was in Italy
recently there was this woman with just about everything 'wrong' with her. Her upper arms were just a
touch too flabby, her clothes were just a bit too tight,
her bra strap was showing and she was wearing these
slipper things in the street and her bottom was *enor-*

mous. On top of all this, she had an apron on (as these Latin women tend to, you know), but by bosoms she was *sexy*. Normally I would have baulked (inwardly, silently) and thought, 'Cor, she hasn't got a clue.' But she radiated something: she was attractive, really attractive, because she was totally confident. I have to admit that for days afterwards I tried to affect this nonchalant mode of dress. Even my husband said she was one of the sexiest women he had ever met (after me, of course). But I digress. Cut-off cardigans are brilliant for you [see previous problem]. If you don't have any, buy cheap ones and cut them off yourself; they should come to just below bust level. The old trick of tying a cardigan or something else around your waist is also a good camouflage trick (make sure it is made of thin material or else you will just bulk yourself out). Vivienne Westwood did, absolutely, make bottoms fashionable. And look at Alexander McQueen's stonkingly sexy tailoring. Didn't you see Kate Winslet at the Oscars and how sexy she looked in one of his Givenchy couture outfits? (If you should ever be interested in McQueen's Givenchy couture, ring the Paris office for more details on 003 314 431 5000.) There are few things sexier than a woman with an hourglass figure.

Recently I lost all my hair due to chemotherapy but I still wish to look nice, both indoors and out. I can only bear to wear a wig for a short while and, at forty-three, turbans make me look too matronly. Square scarves are fun but I can only

find polyester ones in the shops and they slide off easily.
Any ideas? Please don't ask me to go bald disgracefully – it
frightens my son. Thank you. – *Ruth Burrows, Bristol*

I wouldn't dream of telling you to go bald, even
though I think it can look beautiful. I can't imagine
how I'd feel if I lost my hair, even temporarily, but I
can try to understand what a blow it must be to a
woman's self-confidence. I don't want your son to be
frightened either! I turned to the Macmillan Cancer
Relief Fund, who spoke to two specialist nurses in
this field on my behalf. Obviously they deal with
problems such as these every day; they suggested
using cotton scarves, as these don't slip as much as
polyester. (My hint would also be that crêpy fabric –
either silk or synthetic – would be less slippery, as
the surface isn't as smooth.) They also suggested getting a stretchy Alice band and sewing your scarf to it:
i.e., fold the material over the band to cover it, don't
sew it all the way round, slip it on to your head and
then tie the scarf at the back of your neck. Remember
you can also use lengths of material, which you just
need to hem. I know it's a pain sewing, but this will
give you so much more choice. You might also like
to experiment with light cotton hats when spring
comes, but I appreciate that you may feel a little silly
wearing these indoors. I know you don't like the idea
of turbans or wigs, but for the sake of others in this
predicament who would like to try them, Macmillan
also told me about two companies. Lizannes of
Luton Ltd (01323 766894) make turbans and have a
great deal of expertise in this field; they cost £1.50

and members of the public can ring them direct.
Then there is Natural Image Wigs, who supply
department stores. They also make turbans (towelling
£8.50, velveteen £8.50 and polyester £8.50), in various
colours; to find out details of stockists call them on
202 7403 2440, mail order call 020 7403 5588. I really
hope this helps and that you make a speedy and full
recovery.

cooooosy
keeping comfortable and warm and toasty
chic dressing gowns and hot slippers

Help. I have very cold feet and my kittens, Ollie and Stanley, keep biting my toes! In the 1980s my friend Clare had some fab boot slippers which were fur-lined and may or may not have been called Ugg Boots (this is what she called them). They had a semi-hard sole (at least I think so, as I often saw her trotting about outside in them) and I think, for slippers, were quite expensive. Unfortunately, Clare has emigrated to Australia. Do they still exist? Where can I buy some? Please help! – *Sophie Cullinan, Ramsbottom, Bury*

I am hardly surprised that your friend emigrated to Australia if that was the level of your conversation. They are now called Celt Boots, £66, 23 colours, sizes 5–14 and you can get in touch with the Celtic Sheepskin Co. (01637 871605), who will tell you your nearest stockist; there are lots of different styles to choose from. The Celt slippers (which, fabbily, are machine-washable) come in 23 colours, are sized 5–14 and cost £31 (+ £2.50 p&p).

We have recently moved from a cosy London terrace to a draughty, cold heap and I am desperate to find a really WARM dressing gown. I don't want one of those horrid cheap fluffy ones that go bobbly straight away, or anything quilted like my grandma used to wear. I would like wool or wool mix if possible, ideally with a button-up neck rather than wrap-over and neat sleeves rather than huge turn-ups, as these get in the way. Harrods have quoted £300–£500 – the only wool ones I've been able to find so far – too much for me. I could pay up to about £120 or so. Maybe a dressmaker could make me one? – *Sarah Hollis, Sunningdale, Berks*

Well, you certainly could look through the 'Dress-maker' directory on www.dearannie.com if you want to, but otherwise try a winter-weight kimono, in silk or cotton (silk is very warm, remember). Asahi, at 110 Golbourne Road, London w10 5PS, do some beautiful vintage ones from the 1920s–1960s: their bargain bin has ones up to £20, others are up to £70, and you will have something totally original. Call them on 020 8960 7299, as they can also do mail order.

Once upon a time there was a Japanese shop in Brighton and there I once bought a cotton kimono which I have used as a summer dressing gown ever since. It is cool, elegant, easily laundered and WORN OUT. So can you suggest where I might find a replacement before next year's heat wave? – *Brenda Heasman, West Sussex*

You must visit Asahi in London (110 Golbourne Road, London w10 5PS, tel: 020 8960 7299) if you can [see Sarah's letter above]. They specialize in vintage kimonos, with some dating back to the early nineteenth century. They have hundreds of different designs, colours and fabrics: rayon, silk, cotton; and they're all handmade. It is the perfect place for anyone wanting to pick up something slightly different in the dressing-gown department. Cotton ones are more modern but are still not new. Prices start at £15. Bargain! Although, like all lovely things, you have to see them. If you really don't want to make the trip, you can call Asahi up and be really specific about the sort of thing you want and they may be able to satisfy you postally.

I think that the kimono that your correspondent is looking for is actually what the Japanese call a *yukata* – a sort of dressing gown that people are given when they stay at traditional hotels. A kimono is a much more formal garment and not normally washable. I used to live in Brighton and recall the Japanese shop sold both. I have a couple of *yukata*s which were both bought in Japan. If your correspondent wants one, I would suggest that the shops in the Yaohan Plaza, on the Edgware Road in London, are worth a look – it's a large Japanese shopping centre. Do watch the sizing – the Japanese are much smaller than the British. I (at 5'7") bought a men's garment in Japan. I hope this helps. I think your column (and the 'Big Shoe' directory) is great! – *Susie Northfield, Didcot*

Thanks for the very helpful advice, Susie, and the compliments. More please.

dry-cleaning dramas
and wet-cleaning ones too,
as well as dyeing things you're sick of
anything and everything to do
with washing and dyeing

Is there anything in your wide experience that you might be able to bring to bear on the following predicament? My wife bought a very nice silk dress recently. She wore it to a party, and then took it to the dry cleaners. When she went to collect it, it had a horrible stain all down the back where, it would appear, some chemical had been spilt on it. Naturally my wife objected to the state her dress was in but the dry cleaner says it must have been brought in like that; i.e. that my wife had spilt the stuff all over the dress herself. My wife is adamant that this was not the case and that the dress was ruined while in the hands of the dry cleaner. But it's his word against hers, the dry cleaner is absolutely refusing to accept responsibility, so there's an impasse. Any thoughts as to where she goes from here? Is there a dry cleaners' association to whom one can make representations?

Mr S. Sandwich, London

Splendid name. How could I not help, not least because, as I promised last week, it concerns a dry cleaning drama and we all know how I love those at the moment (but no more after this for a while, please!). There is a dry cleaner's association, the Textile Services Association, but not all dry cleaners are members and the TSA can only help if one of their members is involved. If your

dry cleaners is a member there should be a sticker in
the window or you can ring and ask them if you don't
fancy going in again (and who can blame you). My gut
instinct is that they are not. In which case the TSA
advised me that your only real course of redress is
through the small claims court for compensation, or to
visit your local Citizens Advice Bureau. If it turns out
your DC is a member then contact the TSA (020 8863
7755). They offer an arbitration service – i.e. not a
legal service – but they can act as mediators to find out
where the fault lies. If the dry cleaners are at fault the
TSA will instruct them to pay compensation.
Importantly, and fabulously, they have a list of test
houses where garments can be sent for 'material
forensics'!! This helps to find out where the fault lies,
with the DC, with the customer, or maybe even with
the manufacturer. In your wife's case this would be
most useful to find out what the stain is. I hope your
DC is a member; if not, perhaps best consign this to
lessons learnt and all that and in future, only use a
DC that is.

**I got some pollen on my white t-shirt, I tried to brush it off
but that didn't work and despite several washes it won't
come out. Will it ever? – *Kate Shelton, Birmingham***
Unlikely. You could try bleach, which is the only
thing that might get it out. What you should have
done is lift the pollen off with sticky tape. Brushing
just drives it deeper into the fabric. Don't worry, it
was a lesson well learnt on what I hope wasn't a highly
expensive/precious garment.

I have a pair of white leather loafers which I wore quite a lot in the summer, but am loath to get rid of them, even though I know they will be quite passé by next summer. They are still in good repair, so is it sensible to dye them black, to get some winter wear out of them, and if so how would you recommend going about it? They have a 1" heel in pale, varnished wood. – *Susie Thomson, East Sheen*

You are right to dye them. Dyeing, whether it be shoes or clothes, is an easy and cheap way to revitalize your wardrobe and a trick that not enough people make use of. Dylon Shoe Colour make a whole heap of dyes for shoes, in lots of colours to suit leather, synthetic and canvas shoes. It costs £2.55 and gives a long-lasting finish that doesn't crack or peel (they also do a Satin Shoe Colour for £1.99). Dylon have also given me a handy hint to create a mock-croc effect you may like to try, which involves painting the dye over an orange netting bag. As for the heel, this shouldn't look odd. But if you decide you don't like it you could either paint the heels (get one of those little pots from your DIY or art shop, making sure it is suitable for wood), you can stain them with wood stain, or you could try just brushing black shoe polish into them. I find this is sometimes enough to darken the heel. Dylon have a brilliant consumer advice line that can help with any aspect of dyeing shoes or clothes with their dyes (020 8663 4296).

I had a dress made for me and I don't know what to do now that it needs cleaning as obviously it has no care label. – *E. Harper (Miss), Fulham*

Do you remember where you bought the fabric from? If you do, take the dress back to the shop and they may be able to tell you or give you the manufacturer's address to write to for care advice. If you or your dressmaker has scraps of fabric left, you can also take them to any reputable dry-cleaners, who will be able to test the scraps with the different dry-cleaning chemicals they use. If none of the above applies, try a top-class dry-cleaners such as Lilliman and Cox (020 7629 4555), Tothills (020 7252 0100) or Blossom and Browne's Sycamore (020 8552 1231), as they are all very helpful and will be able to advise you.

I have a very favourite suit which feels like corded silk but the fabric is 52 per cent cupro and 48 per cent viscose. It is so comfortable and fits well, but I am not happy with the colour, which is a rather sugary pink. Would it be suitable for dyeing? If so, are there any specialists whom I should contact to carry out the job? If the fabric is unsuitable for dyeing, what would your suggestions be to achieve a different look. It has a knee-length pencil skirt and long-line waisted jacket with short sleeves. – *Elizabeth Willsher, Maldon, Essex*

I keep meaning to get loads of things dyed, but haven't managed to be that organized so far. Now then, Chalfont Dyers and Cleaners, 222 Baker Street, London NW1 5RT, tel: 020 7935 7316, are apparently the people to go to. They will dye clothes and soft furnishings made from natural fibres only (cotton, silk, wool). Customers must send garments to the above address; when the garments have been assessed (age, history, etc.), paperwork will be sent out, as the

customer's signature is required to go ahead with the
job (which takes three to six weeks). There are about
six colours available for clothes and prices vary:
jumpers cost around £40, jeans £35. Their advice about
your suit is that they would never dye structured jackets because the front seams can be too tiny and split in
the delicate process involved. Also linings and inter-
facing cause too many problems. Your skirt (52 per
cent cupro and 48 per cent viscose) can be dyed as
both fabrics come from natural fibres, but both
become limp after the dyeing process, which loses the
'dressing' somewhat. So, in short, best leave it this
time. As for a different look, well . . . what, really?
Wear the jacket with something else? [Look in my
'Dressmakers' directory on my website and then you
can get the suit copied and the dressmaker might be
able to find the same type of fabric for you, but in a
different colour.]

**Why is it that after a few (machine) washes all my white
underwear goes grey? And should I wash my bras by hand?
– *Hermione Phillips, Winchester***
My guess is that you are washing them at too high a
temperature. This is easy to do with whites as you
bung them in the machine at about sixty degrees. They
should really be washed at no higher than fifty degrees
(that ten degrees less makes all the difference), especially if they contain synthetic fibres, as most do
nowadays. If a great deal of your underwear is white,
then it is worth doing them in a separate delicates load
(if your machine has a half-wash button then use that

too if the load is small). Yes, you *should* wash your bras by hand, but who can really be bothered? They are so small and fiddly that you end up scrubbing your hands to kingdom come. And anyway people say you should change your bras every year, so what's the point? My advice is that life is too short to hand-wash anything but the most delicate of apparel. Get a laundry bag (white big netty thing, Johnny Loulou sell them), stick your bras in there, put the machine on and go and drink more gin.

For Christmas my mother bought me a beautiful ivory coloured pashmina, which positively glows and is thoroughly lovely. She has made me promise not to put it away for best but to use it as everyday clothing. Which I am delighted to do, of course. But reality intrudes: I have two small babies and inevitably one of them will puke, poo or throw spaghetti on my beautiful pashmina. When this happens, how on earth do I clean it? It doesn't have a care label and it's made of pashmina and silk. – *Vicky Portman, Cheshire*

You should gently handwash it in warm water using either baby shampoo or Woolite. But, despite having the world's most organised laundry system known to man, my very own pashmina inadvertently went into the washing machine once on a 40 degree delicates wash, under cover of my various fleeces. Not a wool wash, just a delicates wash. And it's as soft and fluffy (and big) as ever it was. So whilst I don't recommend it, the point is that pashminas, like babies, are tougher than we think.

I have a lovely pair of shoes that I bought for my wedding and have not worn since. They are made of a white material that looks like (but isn't) raw silk. I would like to have them dyed a cream colour (if possible) or another colour to go with an outfit (yet to be decided) for a friend's wedding in the summer. How does one set about getting this done?
– *Sian Forbes, Westbury, Wiltshire*

Now then, pay attention, everybody: Julia Taylor dyes shoes any colour (she mixes her own), but you need to post your shoes and a piece of fabric in the desired colour to her. Julia thinks your shoes sound like dupion silk, but would need more specific information to assess whether they can be dyed or not. Anyway, prices start at £50 for synthetic lined shoes, £60 for leather lined (all enquiries to 020 7289 3966).

Last year, while pregnant, I splashed out on a lovely empire-line Ghost dress (£160), which was perfect then. Now, it is far too big for me (it makes me look like a hippie), yet I'd like to get more wear out of it. Also it is white and therefore slightly see-through. I thought dyeing it might also be an option. Will it make the dress shrink? – *I. Pronto (Mrs), Sheffield*

All Ghost clothes are brilliant for pregnant women because they are easy to wear and their style (flowing and empire line, wide trousers and the like) is perfectly suited to a big tummy. They are also infinitely more stylish than most specialist maternity labels, which is why they are always worn by models pre, during and after pregnancy. Although Ghost clothes are meant to be loose, I can understand that perhaps this dress is now too big for you. As Ghost garments are all viscose-based, they are perfect for dyeing. Try Dylon's Machine Dye, which gives excellent results and it's all done in the washing machine (the only extra ingredient you'll need is salt), so there's no mess. It comes in twenty-seven different colours and costs £4.49 from department stores; Dylon have a very helpful consumer advice line if you have any queries (020 8663 4296). The dress will not shrink further as it has already been shrunk in the manufacturing process, although a Ghost representative tells me that excessive tumble-drying might make it shrink slightly! Dye it first and see what happens: a darker colour might help to make it look less voluminous. Otherwise have it altered by a local dressmaker [see 'Dressmakers' directory on www.dearannie.com].

I recently bought a pure-cotton sweater of a good make. Unfortunately, it is a size too big, and as I bought it in a sale and it was the last one I can't return it. Is there any method of shrinking? I don't mind taking a bit of a chance!
– *James, North Yorks*

The only thing you can do is try putting it through a boil wash. But I doubt it will make any difference. Wear it a size too big – it'll look cute and girls will want to mother you. Or send it to Pavarotti, he can use it as a skinny rib.

About six or seven years ago, a dear friend made me buy a straw hat which quickly became indispensable. It is made of very fine and flexible woven straw. It goes with everything I own and never blows off. Unfortunately, it is really looking its age and in need of cleaning. Is there a remedy for this? Please help. – *Catherine Rose, Olney, Bucks*

Apologies for taking so long to reply to this. I spoke to a friendly milliner, Lucy Barlow (45 Buckingham Road, Brighton, BN1 3RQ, tel: 01273 323969), who suggested the following: pad the hat so that it isn't flat and is supported – you can use clean cotton 'rags' or tissue for this. Then get another cotton rag and rub some soap on it (you must make sure that the soap doesn't have bleach in it, otherwise the straw will go yellow – always do a patch test first, as the saying goes) and then gently go over the hat to clean it. Then, with the hat still padded out, put a clean piece of cotton over it and iron the hat. To do this it is really important that the hat is supported and not flat, so with the stuffing in the hat, put one hand in the hat and use the other to press the iron (with the cotton in between hat and iron). As long as you have this fabric to protect your hat, the iron can be quite hot. This will steam your hat back into shape. It is also really important that you don't get the hat too wet, otherwise you will ruin it.

I recently bought a silver-coloured Schott pilot's jacket which cost me nearly £150 – but I thought it was well worth it as it was very warm and comfortable and even, I was told, fireproof. About four weeks later I took it to be dry-cleaned for the first time. When I collected it from the shop it smelt terribly of fried onions and I said it would need to be recleaned. When it came back again it smelt fine. The trouble is that over the last few weeks the fried-onion smell has gradually come back. I can only assume that it has something to do with the dry-cleaning process. What am I to do? If I go out wearing it my friends and colleagues will think that I hang around cheap hamburger stalls. Can you help? – *Iain, London*

I spoke to Schott's head office in New Jersey, USA, who said they don't do a fireproof jacket. Harrods (who stock Schott) said that the fabric content of your jacket is 50 per cent nylon and 50 per cent rayon on the outside, with 100 per cent nylon lining. The padding is 100 per cent polyester fibre-fill. Unusual smells are a common problem when it comes to dry-cleaning complaints. Yours sounds like it is due to a cleaning error, where there had been a chemical breakdown in the solvent used (this would account for the immediate ponginess). Or, as the smell also came back gradually, it could be due to the fabric finish (i.e., manufacturing fault). Either way, try asking your dry-cleaner to use a different machine from the one they used previously. If the problem persists, take the jacket back to where you bought it, explain what has happened and they should send it back to Schott.

I recently bought a lined white linen shift dress. Inevitably someone spilt a drink on it when I wore it to a club. As the care label said 'Dry Clean Only', I took it to TWO dry-cleaners, both of whom said they couldn't do anything about the stain because their stain removers couldn't be used on linen, and they wouldn't recommend washing. Is there anything we can do to salvage this? And isn't it time manufacturers started making clothes that could be worn and washed without major trauma? Or at least provided clear and prominent warnings on their more vulnerable garments? Over the last few months I've had to return at least three garments which have shrunk or whose colours have run, and the assistants look at me as if I'm beneath contempt for even bothering to return items which they seem to think should be worn once and thrown away. – *Jeannette King, Aberdeen*

I agree it is frustrating, but I am not sure what you mean about providing 'clear and prominent warnings on their more vulnerable garments'. Any fabric in white is 'vulnerable' and accidents do, of course, happen. I am astonished that two dry-cleaners said they couldn't help – linen is hardly difficult. I could understand it if you were presenting them with a hand-beaded evening gown! And I have never heard of stain removers not being able to be used on linen; it is a natural fibre and hardly volatile. I spoke to the woman who owns the store your dress is from and she in turn spoke to the Dry Cleaning Technology Centre, which is strictly for the trade and does not deal with enquiries from scussy members of the public. They suggest finding a dry-cleaners that uses Aquatex as a stain remover, which they say is available in better dry-cleaners. I rang the DTC for you to find out a bit more about it and see if they knew of a dry-cleaners that uses Aquatex in your area. They were uninterested in trying to help, saying they were 'rather busy' and put the phone down without so much as a 'I'm a rude pig and no mistake'. Good manners are so important. What hope is there? I have had a few letters about the great dry-cleaning debate and there are certain things that we have to understand. One is that anything with an acetate lining, no matter what the outer fabric is made from, will have to be dry-cleaned. As we strive for newer fabrics and more fancy clothes, we have to accept that they need a different level of care. But if you have cleaned any clothes according to the label instructions and they have shrunk or whatever, complain and don't stop at the assistants. Write to the head office or manager (not to me!) and demand justice.

An apology: In the above letter I mentioned the Dry Cleaning Technology Centre and said that the person who picked up the phone had been most unhelpful and put the phone down without so much as an 'I'm a rude pig and no mistake'. I'd like to apologize unreservedly to pigs everywhere, but especially those on my farm, who since this column appeared have been refusing to roll around in mud and have been snorting at me in a most unappealing fashion. In the light of mad cow disease and reported mad lamb disease, my pigs are a valuable commodity. So Hermès pig collars all round to my herd and soz soz soz.

Please help! My nylon Prada tote bag is beginning to look old and battered. I can't afford a new one (my boyfriend won't give me his credit card), so is there a service where I can get it cleaned and shaped to its original beautiful form? – *Anna, Stoke-on-Trent*

Anna, Anna, Anna, all *sorts* of comments come to mind here: starving children; cures for cancer; hospital waiting lists; old people and broken hips; not enough books in schools; not enough meadows in the countryside; over-population; shrinking ice-caps. Not to mention expecting your boyfriend to cough up. But where would the world be without nylon frippery? Anyhoo,

I rang the Prada shop. I was rather flabbergasted to hear that they DO NOT provide a cleaning or a reshaping service – 'Nothing lasts for ever,' they said. (Miuccia, Miuccia: *che vergonia!* I must have a word with you about this next time we are having pasta e funghi sotto olio together.) They do, however, recommend Scovies (35 Dulwich Village, London SE21 7BN, tel: 020 8693 2755), where they send all Prada clothes and accessories for cleaning (I'm not sure what they mean by this as they don't provide a cleaning service . . .). Scovies clean each bag individually – no dry-cleaning – and this costs £25 for a nylon bag depending on trimmings, etc. No chance of reshaping (apparently bags should be kept like shoes – stuffed when not in use). I also rang the TSA (Textile Services Association) on 020 8863 7755 to find cleaners registered in Stoke, and they had four. So another one to try is the Sketchley Dry Cleaners, 38 Gaolgate Street, Stafford, ST16 2NR, tel: 01785 258908. They will do it if there's a care label which says dry-cleaning is poss. It will cost about £5. If there's any plastic on it they won't because it will be ruined – they recommended bringing it in for them to have a look at. For cleaning purposes you could also try saddle soap. But otherwise it looks like you'll have to flash your boyfie and steal his wallet while he's still in shock.

In Venice in January I bought a pair of super black sheeny-shiny leather shoes. They are, however, definitely NOT patent leather, but I do want to maintain their glossy look and have as yet dared not polish them. Will ordinary polish dull the

leather? Please advise. I remain, your faithful reader. –
Margot Beard, Rhodes University, Grahamstown, South Africa
Meltonian (01753 523971) do some products (All
Leather Shine Aerosol, £3.00, or there's a 'super shine
sponge', £1.55) but these products are only available in
the UK. In South Africa try Kiwi products like Kiwi
Elite Liquid (call them in Natal: 719 7111). Mr White
at posh cobblers John Lobb said that good polish
shouldn't dull the leather and that although it was difficult to say without seeing the leather, if you spend long
enough – sometimes a few hours (!) – then any leather
should polish up, and some traditional cobblers will
polish your shoes for a fee. He gave this advice on
polishing technique: all leather needs feeding, so you
should push in a small amount of leather cream in
small circles, adding a little bit of water as you're going
round as this hardens the polish more quickly and
helps to get a shine faster (like old-fashioned spit and
polish). After you've worked the cream in, leave for ten
minutes and then polish. If you want extra gloss, then
add a wax polish to enhance the shine. Yum.

I was really pleased with myself when I found a Christian
Dior suit in a second-hand shop at a third of its price new.
However, I now find that it picks up stains so easily that I'm
spending a fortune on dry-cleaning. It is bright red and
made of pure new wool. Even a splash of water leaves a
brownish stain that looks like coffee has been spilt on it.
Can you suggest anything? Please keep me anonymous as I
don't think anyone in my office knows I buy second-hand
clothes! – *D., Wiltshire*

Oh, really! What shame is there in buying second-hand clothes? Rather canny and clever, I think! There is nothing I can suggest, *tant pis* (that's French), but what a pain, eh? Probably why someone bunged it in the second-hand shop in the first place. Teflon is now used as a fibre coating to aid in resisting stains but there's not very much you can do with it now . . . sorry. Donate it back to the charity shop and let someone else have the problem. Tee hee.

What is it with dry-clean-only labels? Why the epidemic? Is it laziness or fear of litigation that makes so many manufacturers slap them on even perfectly washable fabrics? Or are they shareholders in the dry-cleaning industry? Is it a sales ploy to make us feel pampered? In any case, they're making a big mistake. I refuse to buy everyday separates which claim to require professional dry-cleaning – unless common sense tells me I can wash them, which it often has. However, I have just bought a beige, dry-clean-only microfibre mac which I'd dearly love to wash but daren't. It's 100 per cent polyester and the lining is 100 per cent acetate. My friend has a microfibre coat she throws into the washing machine. Surely you can't get more washable than pure polyester – or can you? Is there an independent advisory body or person I could ask? Or do you know the answer? And will someone please persuade manufacturers to tell the truth about their fabrics so we can make our own minds up about how to damn well clean them? – *C. Mohr (Ms), London*

There isn't an independent advisory body or person you can ask; it's down to common sense and trial and

error, I'm afraid. I have long suspected that manufacturers stick 'dry-clean' instructions in willy-nilly but
trying to get anyone to admit to it is impossible. I
turned to the Fabric Care Research Association for a
bit of advice. They said that whether a garment can be
dry-cleaned or washed will very much depend on its
total make-up, which must include not only the outer
fabric and the lining, but any interlining, any adorn-
ments such as buttons or trims, and the appropriate
dyestuffs that have been used. (This is why one thing
made out of polyester might be washable and another
won't be.) They advised looking for proper care labels
(i.e., not just 'dry-clean only'). Believe it or not, the use
of care labelling in the UK remains voluntary, so we
are actually lucky to get anything at all. Some things of
course do have to be dry-cleaned, either because of the
fabric or because of the structure (tailored items, things
with linings or shoulder pads, etc.). But while few people mind getting special-occasion clothes dry-cleaned,
it is particularly annoying when you buy something
that you plan to wear extensively – a slip dress or
unlined pair of trousers, for example – only to find it is
dry-clean only. I dry-clean nothing other than coats or
posh stuff and refuse, like you, to buy anything that is
dry-clean only. Of course you *can* wash lots of dry-
clean-only garments perfectly successfully – I have –
but the risk is ours. (Be careful with garments listing
rayon or viscose in them; they can seem perfectly
washable but often shrink, so follow the label instructions carefully here.) I wouldn't wash your mac,
because it's not as simple as saying that this or that

fibre is washable (and polyester is a fibre not a fabric), because it depends on lots of scientific stuff. And as anything with a lining does not tend to take to water, you may find the outer fabric washes well and the lining shrinks, for example. If everyone avoided dry-clean-only clothes wherever possible and *wrote* to the shops and manufacturers to make their point, things might change rather quicker.

My problem is this: how can I bring back the 'puff' back into my 'puffa'? Being a keen all-weather city cyclist, my favoured outer garment is the puffa jacket, which is deliciously warm and practical in the winter. Sadly, however, it seems that after no more than two seasons' use the macho Michelin look evaporates and I am left with a limp rag that hangs and droops dull and lifeless. All of these treasures are goose down-filled and three have a nylon exterior. The most expensive one is a £500 leather Schott puffa, which I am naturally loath to replace. Washing one once in a machine, I have discovered this to be completely ruinous and I doubt that dry-cleaning will rejuvenate them. Is there a cure? How can I reintroduce the zest and spring into my poorly puffas? – *Ken Russell, London*

Are you *the* Ken Russell? Now then, there is a make called Puffa, but this is often used as a generic to describe all those jackets. I called Puffa and they said that if it were a real Puffa then it would be filled with exclusive Puffa down – which is fully machine-washable. Goose down hasn't been used in their jackets for over ten years – they could only suggest taking it to a dry-cleaners for special cleaning advice. I then spoke to the manageress at Hayward Dry Cleaners, 25b Lowndes Street, London SW1X 9JF , tel: 020 7235 4844, who was a delight and said that if you take it in the fabric consultant would look into the possibilities of restuffing (might be worth it for the leather one), but it would depend on technicalities like the stitching, etc. I then rang Schott for a second opinion and they said an interesting thing: put your non-leather jackets in a cool wash (I know you've tried this before but . . .) of forty degrees with a clean trainer in there as well to agitate the wash and fluff up the feathers! But don't tumble-dry. For the leather one just shake it around a lot . . . mmm, not sure about how useful this piece of advice is! You may be interested to know that there are things called Washballs from the fabulous shopping channel QVC (sorry, I won't hear a word against it. Am currently trying to decide whether I really need the 'Pilates Performer' table that they do). They cost £14.98 (plus £2.45 p&p) for two which will last for eighty washloads. Ring 0800 504030 for more details.

sew, sew
making and mending
old stuff becomes new again

Some years ago at a Nicole Farhi sale I bought a skirt and jacket suit with divine pewter fish-shaped buttons. I have now lost one of them and am distraught. Can I find fish-shaped buttons anywhere else? Should I change the whole lot? – *Karen Hamilton, London*

I spoke to Nicole Farhi's office for you and they said that they keep a 'button box' with buttons from past collections, so although they can't promise to have your button you're in with a good chance. Ring the manageress of the Bond Street shop and she'll put you in touch with the appropriate person (020 7499 8368). It is this sort of sterling after-sales service which makes buying British designer clothes worthwhile. Just in case they don't have your button and you decide to change all of them, you may wish to try the Button Queen, 19 Marylebone Lane, London WIM 5FE (020 7935 1505); this shop has a smorgasbord of buttons for you to choose from.

This request is slightly at a tangent to your usual queries, but I hope you'll be able to help. I make most of my clothes and love dressmaking. Thanks to dress making patterns, I could have a wardrobe full of Donna Karan and Issey Miyake,

but finding fabric is depressingly difficult. Liberty is fantastic, but I wonder if you could suggest anywhere a bit closer
to Leeds, or mail-order specialists. I've tried finding shops
through magazine adverts, but without much success. What
I'm after at the moment are wool/Lycra mixes, wool jersey,
cotton duck and trouser-weight linen. Any suggestions
would be greatly appreciated. – *Sue Hamelman, Leeds*

The good news is that Liberty produce a catalogue,
the 'Fabrics Direct' catalogue, which is free, but this
does not have everything in it. For other stuff they can
also provide samples of fabrics if you contact them:
Liberty, Regent Street, London W1R 6AH, tel: 020 7573
9445 (ask for extension 2244 for the mail-order catalogue). John Lewis, Oxford Street, London W1A 1EX,
tel: 020 7629 7711 (ask for dress fabrics), also provide a
spiffing service, which is nothing less than I would
expect of my beloved Johnny Loulou (and no this isn't
an advert). They have a whole department dedicated to
samples! And will send out, free of charge, up to five
samples of fabric if you call and describe the sort of
thing you want. This is for fabric up to £20 per metre;
any fabric costing more than that and you will have to
buy a ten-centimetre piece. When you have decided
what you want, you can order by phone, paying by
Switch or account card (not credit cards). Allans, 75
Duke Street, London W1M 5DJ, tel: 020 7629 5947,
don't have a catalogue but if you write in explaining
what you want, with an SAE, they will then select several suitables and send them out. They keep a note of
the reference number of what they've sent, so if you
decide 'Yes please!' they know what you're referring

to and then you can order and pay by cheque/credit card. Nevtext Interloop Ltd on 0115 959 8781 are mail-order merchants who provide fabrics and trimmings, mostly for dance and theatrical use (they tend to be bright). Prices vary wildly but you can buy whatever amount you want, although it works out cheaper if you buy in bulk. You can send for their free 'top 39 materials' cuttings book and shade guide. Or buy their catalogue for £17.63 which has a swatch of every fabric they stock.

I have a lovely pale yellow cotton jumper with some cabling and decorative ribbing at the cuffs and bottom. But I have been unable to wear it for a while as, despite careful washing, it has stretched to ridiculous proportions. Although still OK in width, its length now reaches my knees and the sleeves flap around about 5" beyond my fingertips. Is there any way I can successfully shorten it again? I am very handy at sewing but to date have been afraid of taking the scissors to it for fear of ruining it altogether. Please don't suggest I wear it as a dress as that would look very silly on me. Perhaps you and your panel of experts can come up with a solution for me?
– *Cathy Sweeny, Dublin*

Why don't you wear it as a dress? Joke! This business of 'you and your panel of experts' – there isn't one, there is just me. I have assistants sometimes, for a few days here and there, but then I miss the research, the detective work, as I track things down and the thrill of it all, and I drive them mad with my nit-picking, 'Have you tried there, or there, or here?' or 'Look in there and through that', and I can see them thinking,

'Do it yourself, then.' So I do. Before you heed my
advice, you must realize that I cannot take responsibility for anything going wrong, OK? The proper way to
do it is to unravel the yarn until it is the length that
you want it to be, then you need to go round with a
crochet hook and secure the stitches. It is impossible
for me to describe this to you (and I don't actually
know how to do it, as my mamma always does it for
me), so I suggest you find a friend who is good with a
crochet hook and get her/him to show you. The other,
very irresponsible thing I've done is cut a jumper, then
with a big needle threaded with some spare yarn that
you take from the severed bit, sew the hem up, catching the stitches as you go. But remember that you will
end up with a plain hem that most probably flares out
because you have removed the rib. As it's a shop-
bought knit, I doubt you will be able to reproduce the
rib yourself by hand-knitting it. Find an old aunt
somewhere, shove it in her direction and give her a
digestive biscuit and a cup of tea. I've been no help at
all, have I?

I have a beloved envelope briefcase that my parents gave me
and it is in very good nick, but the zip is starting to go – the
fabric part is tearing, it is quite old. I love this briefcase but
now use it only for special occasions. Where can I get the zip
fixed? – *A., London*

Although I've never taken anything there myself, a
reader recommended Michael's Shoe Care at
7 Southampton Row, London WC1V 5HA, tel: 020 7405
7436. They also have branches at Ludgate Hill,

Liverpool Street and Fenchurch Street. They repair
zips on bags with prices starting from £24.95.

**I am desperate to find a supply source for a replacement
hand-grip on my suede pigskin attaché case – German manufacture but unspecified, therefore metric size. I understand
that there is a high-quality luggage repairer in London, any
details please. –** *John, Swansea*

Ay, John, you don't like to go in for too much chit-
tie-chat, do you? Very to the point and curt. Hope
you're not like that when chatting up prospective
romantic partners. Selfridges in London's Oxford
Street (020 7318 3657 takes you direct to luggage
repair) have a luggage repair concession in store that
has been there for going on two and ten year and it is
very popular. They said that in principle they could
do it but in practice they'd have to see it. They have a
lot of handles in stock but they'd have to find the
right size and the right colour for the case. There is a
£10 minimum charge for fitting and *sometimes* this
£10 also includes the handle; it depends on what you
want. Generally, prices depend on lots of things that
are quite frankly too boring to go into here and handles start at £15 (you can, if you wish, just buy the
handle and fix it yourself if you come over all practical). If they have your handle in stock, then they can
fix it the same day; if they don't they can order it
from abroad (Italy or wherever) and this obviously
takes a little more time. Michael's Shoe Care,
7 Southampton Row, London WC1V 5HA, tel: 020 7405
7436, said they would need to see it but it would cost

from about a tenner for fitting and a handle. If they
don't have a match, then it's a different quote and
they can try to get one or make one . . . phew.
Handles, what a bloody nightmare, eh? Take care
of yours, readers.

**Can you tell me where I can buy fake fur by the metre to cov-
er a coat collar? Thank you. –** *E. Scott, Edinburgh*
For goodness' sake, have you looked anywhere? I do
think some of you just use me as some sort of servant!
Come on now. Fake fur is sold just about anywhere
and everywhere, you lazy sod. But, because it's nearly
Christmas and as I write I am munching on an early
boozy mince pie (my husband makes them far too
alcoholic, hic), I shall help you. Johnny Loulou have
all sorts from tiger print in gold, cheetah print in grey
with black spots to plain black and brown. The plainer
ones start at £20 per metre. You have a branch in in
the St James Centre, Edinburgh (0131 556 9121), so
go have a look.

BIG . . . small
and in-betweeny sizes
*of all manner of things: clothes,
shoes, bikinis . . .*

I have a real problem finding trousers to fit, so much so that I have lived in leggings for years. I have tried everywhere; not even the designer labels are any good. I have a fairly average figure (size 14), but I am hollow-backed, so that if they fit me around the hips, they are hopelessly big around the waist. I long to be able to wear smart trousers. Do you know of any designer or shop whose trousers might fit me? – *T. Baxter (Mrs), Luton*

This a widespread problem, mostly because the most crucial fit in trousers – the crotch – is rarely measured. Stephen Gray, Professor of Communications and Computer Graphics at Nottingham Trent University, may be the man to change all this. He has brought a measuring booth to this country from France called the Telmat. At the Nottinghamshire International Clothing Centre in Hucknall you can have every part of you measured in 3D for £5 a time. In time he hopes that designers and stores will use his findings to reassess people's measurements (to be really futuristic, he thinks one day our measurements will be stored on smartcards and via a PC you will be able to find out what stores make clothes that fit you the best). In the meantime, have a pair made for you. I can highly

recommend a couturier dressmaker called Olney
Originals (01234 241440) who are not a million miles
from you (they will also travel to London for meetings
with their clients). They can source the fabric for you
if you wish, and will make up a toile (the same garment but in calico) before they go ahead and make the
item in the proper fabric. Three to four fittings ensure
a perfect fit. Prices obviously vary according to the
style and fabric that you choose, but as a guide a pair
of simple tapered trousers in a wool-mix crêpe would
cost £180. Considering how comfortable and flattering
a well-fitting pair of trousers can be, this is actually
very good value for money. [Others should look at the
'Dressmakers' directory on www.dearannie.com to get
the details of a dressmaker nearer home.]

Can you help me track down Little Women, the company that
used to do small sized bras by mail order? The only number I
have for them is defunct. I hope they haven't gone out of
business? – *Tara B., Andover*
No they haven't. You can reach them on 01455 285511,
or via their website: www.littlewomen.co.uk

I am a size 8 or sometimes even 6, depending on the cut.
This makes me the butt of endless 'lucky you' etc comments
which I know are meant nicely but I have real problems
finding clothes that fit. And I daren't complain (hence the
made up name). I particularly have problems with my bottom
half as I have almost no hips. Would you know of a
label/designer/shop that may be good for me and that I may
not have thought of? – *Tallulah, Wales*
Although I have absolutely nothing in common with

you I do sympathise. I get quite a lot of letters from women who are petite and they get really fed up at not being able to buy clothes. You should join the Size 8 Club, which offers a very supportive service, publishing newsletters etc. (where other members' findings are published, so everyone pools their info). Membership costs £25 a year which is refundable against purchase (they produce a small range of their own designed clothes). Call them on 01789 842307 for more details, or have a look at the website: http.//freespace.virgin .net/helena.lomax. Labels you may not have heard of which are good: Miss V, Valentino's diffusion line which starts at an English size 6 (direct enquires to Valentino's head office tel: 00 39 06 67 311). Episode is another good label; their range starts at size 4 up to size 16, call 020 7885 8500 for your nearest stockist. Talbots (sizes 4–20) do a good petites range which is a scaled-down version of their 'main range', call their 24 hour line in the States 001 781 740 8888 for a catalogue. La Redoute, that fab mail-order catalogue, have clothes that start at size 6, call: 0500 777 777.

I've just found out that I am expecting my first baby. Having spent all my adult life striving for a reasonable level of style, a preliminary look at what's available in maternity wear has left me thinking that I'll have to go into solitary confinement for six months. I've been unable to find any specialists in my immediate area and should be extremely grateful if you could advise on mail-order companies or other retailers catering for mums to be. – *L. Strange, Wigan*

This is a real problem for a lot of women. Who decided that pregnant women develop a penchant for large bows and polka dots? But there are some things that can make your life easier, such as maternity tights and leggings; other than that you don't need to go near a maternity shop unless you want to. OK, the sensible advice first. Blooming Marvellous are one maternity mail-order company that do a good range of basics (call 020 8391 4822 for a catalogue). They often also do a starter kit of some sort: e.g., dress, T-shirt and leggings in winter; shorts, T-shirt and vest in summer – that sort of thing. Lots of their styles are really quite simple and not bad at all. Dorothy Perkins also do maternity wear (enquiries: 0800 731 8284), as do H&M (enquiries: 020 7323 2211), so look out for local stores. One other company, Formes, that have been going for just over three years in this country, are a cut above the rest. The clothes are designed and manufactured by Formes, so they all go together. They have three shops in London (and branches in Guildford, Manchester, Nottingham, Edinburgh and Glasgow). There is also a mail-order catalogue (call 020 8689 1122). Their party wear is excellent – stylish and classy, just like 'normal' party wear but for pregnant wimmin. But throughout my pregnancies I didn't wear one piece of maternity wear. Depending on what I was doing, I wore really tight Lycra T-shirts a couple of sizes bigger than I normally would with, say, one of my husband's old shirts left undone (very art-teacher-ish) over the top; little A-line silk slips from Fenwicks and Knickerbox; or little floral summer dresses (if poss empire line), with biker boots and my cut-off

sweaters; devore shirts (Boden) over silk/satin pyjama
bottoms with drawstring waists; stretch velvet dresses.
I also had this shirt which I loved and as it got tighter I
slit the sides to make them look like side vents, just to
make it last a bit longer (it easily sewed back up again
afterwards). Basically I wore whatever I wore normally, but bigger or adapted slightly. I know it's not easy –
some women put weight on all over – but hopefully
one of the companies/solutions I have listed will help
you. Good luck.

I am a fifteen-year-old schoolgirl with a bikini problem. I
spent the whole of last year looking for a bikini, rather
unsuccessfully. I appear to be having the same luck this
year. My problem is that I am a 34C but require only size 8
bottoms. Do you know of anywhere that sells bikini separates, preferably in the West Midlands area? I would be prepared to spend up to £50.
– *Naomi Geffen, West Midlands*
This is such a widespread problem because you will
find that people either make cupped swimwear (i.e. a
34C rather than just a catch-all 34) *or* sell tops and bottoms separately. This is all covered comprehensively
in the 'Swimwear' directory on my website:
www.dearannie.com

I am 5'6" and a size 18–20. The 20 comes on top as I am very
busty. I am totally bored with most clothes in larger sizes, as
they either seem to swathe you in layers of shapelessness or
make you look like a hideous bossy person working in a
building society with no taste. Skirts and trousers aren't too
much of a problem, but I would love to find somewhere that

sells nice tops and jackets that would celebrate my magnifi-
cence rather than try to make me look like a trainee nun. As I
play football and swim, I am a nice curvy shape. My partner
adores me and has threatened to tie me down and force-feed
me Häagen-Dazs if I go on a diet, but is also very interested
in funding some new clothes. We regularly travel quite a bit
around the UK, so distance is no object. I already enjoy
spending lots of money on hats, shoes, etc. and really love
nice things. Any ideas? – *Elizabeth, Plymouth*

With all this talk of foreplay and ice-cream, HD might
well sign you up to star in their next commercial. You
sound like a glorious woman – my husband wants
your phone number. This bigger-size business really
makes me cross, I get so many letters like yours and I
can tell it's a real problem not being able to find nice
clothes. A reader from Bath wrote me the most brilliant letter (thank you) full of good advice, which I
shall pass on; not all of it will be relevant to your
problem but I am sure there are many others it will
help: 'There is one absolute gem of an undies shop
worth a trip from miles, Perfect Fit, 50 Temple Street,
Keynsham (west of Bristol), tel: 0117 986 0950. Their
bras go up to 50H in soft bras and 38J in underwired
and if, like me, you need a bit of tummy support even
the all-in-ones go up to 44DD. There is also Margaret
Ann (01985 840520), who works from home and can
get lusciously enormous undies/swimwear direct from
Germany and Scandinavia, where it is not a disgrace to
be buxom. Two of my favourite shops for the tall, big
and bold are Base, 55 Monmouth Street, London WC2
(020 7240 8914) – they have really smart designs for

large and tall business girls – and Ken Smith's Designs
at 6 Charlotte Place (off Charlotte Street, London w1,
tel: 020 7631 3341) – they are always so welcoming in
there.' Some other readers recommend Magnum in
Hants (01489 891900), which stocks sizes 16–28.
[Also, of course, you must look at the 'Size 16 Plus'
directory on my website: www.dearannie.com, which
is stuffed full of fab places that stock nice clothes in
sizes larger than a size 14.] Finally, on the subject of
hats, have you seen Philip Treacy's sublime designs?
They are breathtakingly expensive, but if you're interested call for an appointment on 020 7259 9605. He
also does a much cheaper line for Debenhams.

*P.S. It was this letter that prompted me to create the 'Size 16
Plus' directory, which has proved to be enormously popular.
And, thanks to that reader in Bath, I discovered the truly fab-
ulous Margaret Ann, who holds one of the coveted 'Dear
Annie' gold stars [see 'Gold Stars' chapter]. And Häagen-
Dazs did get in contact and sent the lovely Elizabeth lots of
vouchers for free ice-cream!*

I have just discovered the only place I knew I could rely on to
cater for my size 9½ feet has been taken over and will not be
making any summer styles to fit me! Have you any suggestions? I'm not that fussy really, as long as I can wear something. It helps if it fits, flatters and is comfortable. I've
trawled around a few places for suitable men's items that
aren't too gruesome or clumpy but no luck yet. – Diana
Pasek-Atkinson, Nottingham

Thank you for the drawings of your feet, side view
and top view, and all your compliments which

modesty has made me edit out of your letter. I have
picked your problem to publish but I have had hundreds of letters from people with the same problem so
it's obviously widespread, and such is the level of
research I have done into this subject that I cannot
possibly print all I have found here. What I am doing
is compiling a bit of a directory thing [. . . which is
just what I did, and the 'Big Shoe' directory can be
found at www.dearannie.com]. There is also a
'Footwear for Special Needs' booklet from the British
Footwear Association, which costs £3 (020 7580 8687).

Clothes enable you to express personality – don't they?
Help, I'm having a hard time being myself at present! Can
you assist? I am 5'10" and a 12/14 with an inside-leg mea-
surement of 34". Despite a creative and broad-minded
approach to shopping, I can't find trousers to fit. All the
retailers who are now doing longer lengths – M&S, Oasis,
Next, etc. – aren't hitting the mark. Long Tall Sally use
cheap materials and tend to design like tall means wide.
So what is a girl to do? Are there any British designers/
labels I've omitted from trials or should I expand my shopping horizons and go to New York to seek out unfinished
'pants', or Europe to find longer brands? Please don't be
deceived into thinking I love shopping – I'm just keen to be
clothed as I wish. As yet I haven't won the Lottery, so my
price range is not going to be in the hundreds. I do have
your dressmakers list but until the ready-to-wear angle is
exhausted I don't want to go down this route. One last
thought: what do those super, and not so super, models do
for limb-covering togs – surely not all made-to-measure?

Hoping you can help. – *Sarah Morrison, south Leicestershire*
Well, models wear expensive designer gear, don't
they? Gucci, for one, make long, long trousers; some
come unfinished, so length isn't really a problem. You
would need a 42 or 44 Gucci (call them on 020 7629
2716 for your nearest stockist.) The Boden catalogue
do 34" unfinished velvet jeans, two styles, £50 and £58
(call 020 8453 1535 for a catalogue). La Redoute have
trousers in two and sometimes three lengths – under
5'7", between 5'7" and 5'9" and over 5'9"; Taillissime
also do trousers for over 5'9" (call 0500 777 777 for a
catalogue from both La Redoute and Taillissime). And
lots of readers have in the past recommended Racing
Green (0990 411 1111) as being very good for people
with long legs and arms; they do an extra-long leg
length on their trousers. STOP PRESS! At the time of
going to press I was busy researching/collating the
Long Legs directory, so please check my website:
www.dearannie.com periodically for the results.

that told you
short shrift for silliness
*for those that really should
have known better*

I am in dispute with my friend as to what the best watch to have is, she says Rolex and I say Cartier. Who is right? –
Simone Frasier, London

Best? What do you mean by best? They are both brilliant watches and won't give you a moment's trouble other than possibly inspiring muscly men to cut your wrists off at traffic lights. If you and your friend have nothing better to argue about, then perhaps a spell in a soup kitchen might give you both something to think about. Of course, if you want to know what's really super-in, then the answer is a black plastic Casio watch from Argos for £20. It's water-resistant to 200 metres, which, divided by 200, should just about be level with you and your friend's IQ (combined).

I have a pretty good figure with a touch of cellulite on my upper thighs. I am going on holiday with some new friends to the Virgin Islands and I am keen to impress. I'd like to know about some good expensive swimsuits that have one of those little skirts attached that would disguise this.
– Kathryn Hart, Hampshire

I'm not sure what you seriously expect me to advise you. Chanel/Ralph Lauren/Donna Karan have done some fantastic swimsuits that will spare your embarrassment? Maybe they have, but you have a pretty good figure and a bit of cellulite. Sod it and show it off. Do you really care? Do your friends really care? Remember that starving people do not have the *luxury* of cellulite. Cellulite is due to too much good living and not enough exercise and I don't give a toning-table toss who says otherwise. Donate your holiday to a good cause, get off your butt and get it moving. But I doubt you'll do any of these. So why not stick £50 notes over the offending area. That way people will know you are filthy rich and will be too bothered being your new best friends to notice a bit of podge.

My girlfriend has the ability to combine sober, sensible clothes with something a bit more frivolous, frilly and playful without looking tasteless or overdressed. She has great legs and prefers to wear stockings when the hem length of her skirt allows it. I've bought her a white skirt and want to buy her some stockings to go with it. I'm thinking of some with a swirly lace pattern or a glittery seam or anything that has a bit of life to it. Fishnet stockings come to mind but there's always something a bit cheesy about them to my mind. I find the hosiery section in department stores a bit daunting with (to the untrained eye!) row upon row of basically the same colours made by different firms. Can you help me with any suggestions as well as the names of manufacturers so at least I'm armed when I next visit a department store. If the answer lies in a specialist shop in London please mention that as I visit London fairly regularly.
– *Martin Forrester, Chorlton*

My dear boy. I know that some people feel that
ladies and gentlemen of the press can have too much
power, expressing, as they do, feelings and opinions
that may influence many. But if I achieve one thing
through this column it will be the eradication of
swirly lace tights. They are foul things that should be
foisted upon only the most unfortunate of women,
perhaps as a punishment for adultery, in countries
that still punish for such things. If you love your girlfriend – nay, boy, even if you *like* her, do not, I beg
you, buy her novelty tights. Words like frivolous,
playful and frilly may come to your mind, but words
such as naff, passé and Molly Ringwald in *Pretty in
Pink* are the only words that come to mine. Forgive
me this violent opinion and let us get on with guiding
you around the hosiery world. The best specialist
shop for hosiery in London, in my opinion, is Fogal.
But they are expensive. There is a branch at 36 New
Bond Street, London W1Y 9HD, tel: 020 7493 0900,
and they have a brilliant array of tights, from boring
but excellent opaques and sheers to something a bit
more 'novelty'. Then you might want to pop into
Fenwick, just up the road at 63 New Bond Street
(020 7629 9161), and then John Lewis and Selfridges
on Oxford Street. The brands to look for are
Jonathan Aston, as they are well known for more
fancy hosiery (in fact they have a red lacy pair if you
really want), and Wolford, for something unusual
such as their seamless tights (Fatal), and, yes, they do
netty/lacy tights. You are sure to find something
among all that lot.

Note: The following season, fancy, lacy tights became the height of fashion, so I guess that told me.

I have hair that hangs lank. I achieve height and curl with an electric brush, then add lacquer to keep the style up. But any hat or headscarf, once on, depresses all the height and I emerge utterly flattened when I take it off. Any suggestions? – Mrs Le Cornu, Jersey

Well, nothing would keep your hair bouffed if you put something on it. It's like asking a soufflé to stay souffléd if you rest a dinner plate on it. Lummy, love, I wish I could suggest some magic Annie trick but I can't. There are only two solutions: don't wear anything on your head or adopt a flatter hairstyle.

I long to see my wife in a thong. I have bought her a few, but she complains that none of them is comfortable. Can you suggest one that is? Also, what is the difference between a thong and a G-string? – Simon, Southampton

There is no difference between a thong, G-string, or string-back pant, as they are also called. They *are* uncomfortable, although some women do like them and they have their place (brilliant for banishing VPL). But if your wife doesn't like wearing one, then that must be her choice. You try wearing one, sunbeam, and then you'll see why your wife doesn't want to.

Meows, dear Annie! You may be wondering why a cat is writing to you, but I do enjoy your column each week. My humans think I'm just washing myself while I sit on the paper and stop them from reading it, but really I'm taking in every word! Anyway, I'm the cause of one of their problems and I wonder if you could help. Since humans don't have thick fur coats like me, they have to wear woollen suits and coats to keep themselves warm, and the trouble is my fur clings to their clothes (along with other threads and dog hair) and is very difficult for them to remove. The worst colours affected are navy blue and black, although red and green also seem to attract hair and my fur, and also miscellaneous 'bits'. Please do you have any suggestions as to how my humans can remove fur and other clinging items from their clothes? They have tried Sellotape (effective, but fiddly and time-consuming), a clothes brush (no use at all) and a rubber glove (this seems to be the best yet), and also storing their clothes in protective covers, but still the fur sticks! If you could find a solution, I would be most grateful, and so would my humans. By the way, my humans live in Exeter in Devon. Purrs . . . – *Otis Baker, via e-mail*

Well, Otis, your humans seem to have tried everything I would have suggested. But you seem like a nice cat, so if you really, really want to be of help to your humans and stop your no doubt cuddly fur sticking to their clothes, then I'd go out and get myself lost if I were you.

This prompted lots of people to write in, but the funniest by far was the following:

As a regular reader of your column, along with my mum, I was rather distressed by your curt treatment of Otis Baker regarding the 'fur on clothes' problem. We cats have to endure this affliction, and it can cause us distress when we are not cuddled by our parents because they are wearing dark clothes. It's a wonder that more of us don't end up seriously disturbed. As everyone around me understands,

I have an opinion on – and know – everything, so of course I have the answer to the problem. Lakeland Ltd (015394 88100)make a product called Sticki-Mitts, ref. 8945, £1.95 for twenty. They are wonderful and my parents use them all the time. The clothes roller, ref. 8913, £6.95, is good too and I have seen these at Johnny Loulou, which is also my mum's favourite shop! Incidentally, in my opinion Mum spent rather too long reading the article on men's pants today in the *Independent on Sunday*'s fashion pages. She is a teacher of more than fifty and should be past all 'that'. Ralph, my brother, now wants a pair of the Hugo Boss ones. – *Katie Austoni, Huntingdon*

Hilarious. Loads of people wrote in to recommend the same. And I thoroughly recommend Lakeland Ltd; they make lovely, useful products and are so helpful. One final note: Lottie, an e-mail correspondent, wrote in to suggest using those green scouring pads; used dry apparently they pick up cat hairs like magic (but don't get confused and use it later for washing up – that would be disgusting).

Annie, sweetie. I think you have a wonderful job, darling, going out shopping with other people's money and having babies occasionally. The rest of us wage slaves can only writhe in green-eyed jealousy. Anyway, I am after something cheap and cheerful which has now died a death and been down-sized to dusting. It is a soft T-shirt-material, off-the-shoulder top with three-quarter-length sleeves and has a knitted welt on the bottom and around the top. I know it sounds naff but I wore it with jeans or jazzed it up with skirt and heels and managed to score nearly every time I went out in it, so it's part of my men-slaying wardrobe. It was so versatile and I feel that I can never go out again if I don't get a replacement for it! I don't mind long sleeves but I would like black. I paid about £15 for it in a cheap little boutique, but despite extensive searches since – nothing. Money around £30 would be nice. Thank you for trying! – *Michelle Varney, East Midlands*

Michelle, sweetie. It's a little more complicated than 'going out shopping with other people's money and having babies occasionally', darling. Perhaps when you outgrow your *penchant* for off-the-shoulder tops, you will understand. Until then, do your own donkey-work. Eeeeor ooooor.

ablative

in latin the ablative is the
'kitchen drawer' of cases, where the
things that have no other natural home go
*a mélange of bits and bobs: where to find
cotton clerical shirts, Spanish fans,
old-fashioned school satchels,
skate gear, etc., etc., etc.*

I keep reading of knee boots, but where can one get boot trees to keep them looking good? I can't find them anywhere.
– *Kitty Hanning, Crystal Palace*

Johnny Loulou do some for £10. Another place to look is antique shops, as they often have the most beautiful old-fashioned wooden ones. And you are right, boot trees and shoe trees should really be used to keep one's posher footwear in tip-toe condition.

Where can I get velvet jeans from? – *Emma Bennett, London*
The mail-order company Boden (020 8453 1535) do a lovely pair, in sizes 8–20, in various colours that change seasonally.

My partner and I are street flower-sellers in Manchester city centre. We provide a range of diverse and high-quality flowers. We have been saving for the past six months for new wardrobes. Our budget is limited to around £1,000, but we understand we can slowly extend our wardrobe over the years by specializing in a definite image. We shall be in London in early February and wish to know where we can buy quality second-hand 1930s–1950s suits, or second-hand designer clothes, unusual and exotic accessories, especially cravats, cufflinks, shirts and shoes. Alternatively, we know a

good tailor in Manchester who with the right material will
make suits to our specifications. Where are there drapers'
shops with an exciting and unusual range of suit cloth?
– *Gerard McDermott and Bennett Mott, Manchester*

When I'm next in Manchester I shall call on you and
pick up some flowers, which I hope you will give me
a jolly big discount on. Shops to visit for all your
requirements: Steinberg and Tolkein, 193 King's Road,
sw3 (Sloane Square tube, near Chelsea Register
Office), tel: 020 7376 3660; Cenci, 31 Monmouth
Street, wc2 (Covent Garden tube), tel: 020 7836 1400,
then try Blackout II, 51 Endell Street, wc2 (also
Covent Garden tube), tel: 020 7240 5006; High
Society, 46 Cross Street, n1 (Highbury and Islington
or Angel tube), tel: 020 7226 6863; Crazy Clothes
Connection, 134 Lancaster Road, w11 (Ladbroke
Grove tube), tel: 020 7221 3989; and lastly, Bertie
Wooster, 284 Fulham Road, sw1 9en (Earl's Court
or Fulham Broadway tube), tel: 020 7352 5662. As for
fabric shops, try Berwick Street, w1 (Oxford Circus
tube), as they have a few good shops; Harrods
(Knightsbridge tube), Selfridges (Marble Arch or
Bond Street tube) and Liberty (Oxford Circus tube) –
then go on to Berwick Street, as it's just round the
corner. [For more hints on fabric, have a look in the
'Sew, Sew' chapter.]

My girlfriend has lovely long hair but cannot find a decent
bathing cap to wear in our municipal swimming pool. Unlike
most women, she wants to protect her hair from the chlorine
in the water which gives her split ends and ruins its fine

nature. Most bathing caps are old-fashioned and make her look like a pinhead! The ones on sale in the baths in machines (no not THOSE machines) are thin and designed for women with perfect oval features – or mannequins. They don't really flatter her. She wants a cap that will give her a bit of height on the top of her head. Colour/pattern are less important. Bathing caps do not seem to have kept pace with other sportswear or swimwear. As you can see at any pool, most women put style before haircare and simply do not wear a cap at all. Any ideas? – *Richard Lysons, Bury*

I cannot tell you how stylish *I* look in my Speedo silicon cap, high-necked swimsuit and mirrored goggles, and I put performance before how I look any swimming day of the week. I can't help thinking it's a bit naff to worry that much about how you look when you swim. Most swimming caps make people look like they have a pinhead – to get height, one must wear synchronized-swimming-style hats with lots of frou-frou flowers (and isn't that just another way of looking ridiculous?). For something a bit different, try some of these shops: Lilywhites, London W1 (020 7915 4000), and Mundy Sports, London N10 (020 8444 7000); for vintage ones, try Delta of Venus (020 7387 3037) and Greenwich Market. My hunch is that she'll find what she wants from vintage shops – she'll have to hunt around though.

Pierced noses, navels, eyebrows and increasingly lips and cheeks are commonplace these days. I had my navel pierced a few years ago and have taken up my previously failed search of finding something other than rings or bars for my

pierced belly-button. I'm sure lots of people with pierced
body parts would be keen to have new and different pieces in
the same way that we all like to change our earrings, rings
and necklaces. The distinct lack of choice also applies to
practical body jewellery. Everyone with a pierced navel has
suffered bouts of inflammation and I believe this is due to
clothing catching on jewellery which is bulky and can easily
cause infection. Do you know of anywhere that specializes in
body jewellery, or somewhere that will design and make jewellery out of surgical steel for my purposes? – *Jeannette
Crockett, London N7*

The Wildcat Body Collection do all sorts of ready-
made nice stuff and they do a catalogue, so write to 16
Preston Street, Brighton, East Sussex BN1 2HN, or tele-
phone on 01273 323758, saying for what part of the
body you need jewellery. Their products are made of
surgical steel, 18ct gold or niobium, which is a
hypo-allergenic material that comes in different
colours and does not affect the skin. Jess James, 3
Newburgh Street, London W1V, tel: 020 7437 0199,
13 Lowndes St, London SW1, tel: 020 7235 7171
(www.jessjames.co.uk) will make things up for you
wherever technically possible, 18ct gold or platinum,
but not surgical steel. Prices start at £120. Finally, Into
You, 144 St John Street, London EC1V 4UA, tel: 020
7253 5085, can also make things up to your own
design in 18ct gold or white gold; prices start at £60.
Nobody I spoke to recommended surgical steel for
your own designs, but I hope that the places I've
mentioned will open up more choice for you.

I am having a few problems finding American-type 'skate gear' and was hoping you could help. I am a sixteen-year-old girl and a size 6–8. I live in Preston but will travel to Manchester or near by. I will also be visiting London some time soon. I would be so grateful if you could inform me of stockists in these areas as I desperately need some new clothes for summer. Pleeease help! – *Suzanne Marsden, Bamber Bridge, Preston*

Exit (41–45 Oldham Street, Manchester M15 1JG, tel: 0161 832 4028) stocks 'hardcore' skate labels, straight from America, including Emerica, Globe, Shortys, Soochi, Toy Machine, Alien Workshop and World Industries. The small size would be right for you. In London the place to go is Slam City Skates (16 Neal's Yard, WC2, tel: 020 7240 0928, Covent Garden tube), which stocks Stussy, Volcon and Fresh Jive for girls. If you can't get there in person, they do a mail-order service if you know exactly what you want, and you'll also need your ma or pa's credit card (yeah!!); p&p varies depending on what is being sent (*c.* £3 for a T-shirt). Before I get complaining letters, I am aware that these are big prices for a teenager, but skate gear is expensive. OK?

This request is so pathetically ordinary that only desperation makes me expose myself to ridicule by sending it. Where can I buy well-made, elegant silk, cotton or linen shirts in bright jewel or pastel colours? Not browns, not oranges, not sludges of any hue, not big overshirts – just tailored shirts to wear with suits? I have shopped in Knightsbridge, Bond Street, Oxford Street – not to mention the Boulevard

Saint-Germaine and the entire 6th arrondissement. You are
my last hope. – *Christine, via e-mail*

Well, Christine, I have left your surname off to save
you ridicule, although none is warranted. Thomas
Pink do a label called 'Ladies' fitted' in four colours,
including light green and white, which are available mail
order, tel: 020 7498 3882, and have stores in Jermyn
Street, London SW1Y 6JD, and others in London,
Dublin, Edinburgh and Glasgow including one dedicated to women's shirts: Thomas Pink Woman, 161 Sloane
Street, London SW1, tel: 020 7730 5967. If you want my
advice, though, Chrissie, and you obviously do, get the
bugger made for you. (See my Dressmakers directory at
www.dearannie.com).

Summer approaches and yet again I'll be facing the same
problem that crops up every year. Does anyone manufacture
anti-perspirant that really doesn't leave white marks on your
clothes? Am I the only woman who wears dark coloured tops
in summer? I've tried several makes like Sure, Secret Stick
and Vaseline Intensive Care who all claim not to leave any
white residue, but no luck. Please help!
– *Jacqueline, Nottingham*

Summer? I see no summer, but as I write this I am
wearing a vest (Gap, last year's) because I'm boiling.
Right then Jacqueline, anti-perspirants. Should we even
be wearing them? So much bad press of late on them . . .
that they block sweat ducts, that they introduce huge
amounts of aluminium into our systems. All the ones
you have been using are in my experience, crap. What I
have found to be good is Secret Satin Dry Cream which

costs around the £2.99 mark and you can get it in Boots,
Superdrug, supermarkets etc. – I think its the only one
that delivers the goods. The stick they do, as you've
found, still leaves a residue on clothes. [Note: after this
appeared, other readers wrote in to recommend the
deodorant stone, £5.20 by Neals Yard Remedies, tel: 020
7627 1949 for details of your nearest stockist, or 0161
831 7875 for mail order. And Trust, which is available
from places like Boots for around £8, which sounds a
lot but you only apply it a couple of times a week.]

I am desperate for an old-fashioned school leather satchel.
I want the kind with a shoulder strap and two pockets at the
front. It must be big enough to hold an A4 folder (preferably
two). Please can you help me, as I have absolutely no idea
where to buy one. If you could I would be eternally grateful!
– *Rachel Tomlinson, Cowbridge, South Wales*
Aren't they lovely, those old leather satchels? Some
flash bag designers do posh versions of them that can
run into thousands, but if you want a good old-fashioned one, then go to any of Johnny Loulou's stores
(such as Peter Jones). In their luggage department (and
sometimes in schoolwear) they do leather satchels
with two front pockets. I don't know if it would be
big enough to take your files, but I guess you could
always pop down with your files and do a bit of sur-
reptitious stuffing. They cost £33. Eden's, a specialist
schoolwear shop in Talbot Green (01443 223387),
were nice and helpful. They said that they can get
what you want from a leather-goods maker who sup-
plies their two shops; prices start at £59.99, but they

reckon they can get exactly the right thing, so it's
worth giving them a call.

This is not strictly a fashion problem but I would be grateful
if you can offer any help. I am trying to find a hanging clothes
bag in which dresses or suits can be transported on their
hangers and will take half a dozen or so garments. Any ideas
about where I might look? – *Mrs J. Campbell, London*

I know what you mean. Johnny Loulou do smaller
hanging bags, as do lots of other places, but not one that
holds lots. Morplan are suppliers to the trade of all
things to do with retail and ordinary mortals can also go
in and buy from their shop at 56 Great Titchfield Street,
London WIP 8DX. Enquiries: 0800 435333. They have a
few suitables. Look at their 'All-Weather Repsacs'
(holds up to 25 garments, in long, slim or short 39"
length, from £75.95 exclusive of VAT). Or they have a
canvas version, 'Economy Repsacs', which cost from
£33.99 for a short 38" length to £41.50 for long 66"
(prices again exclusive of VAT).

gold stars
awarded for the very best

Gold Stars are the fashion equivalent of the Michelin stars. They go to people, shops and labels that I have personal experience of for being excellent; the entries explain in more detail exactly why. This chapter uses very varied problems to introduce the Gold Star holder and it is not arranged in any particular order. Gold Star holders are all equally brilliant and no higher accolade can be granted.

I'd like to buy my girlfriend an engagement ring, but haven't a huge amount of money. I don't want to buy her one of those tiny diamonds but thought you could recommend something unusual to make up for my lack of money! – *Tom de Victor, London*

Oh, you sweet man for not just going and buying some apple-pip diamond from Argos and giving it to her over a Harvester dinner. Sure, it's nice to have a stonking diamond on your finger, but it's also nice to have enough money to pay the rent and buy tea-bags. **The Gold Star award here goes to Jess James,** 3 Newburgh Street, London w1, tel: 020 7437 0199, and 13 Lowndes St, London sw1, tel: 020 7235 7171 (www.jessjames.co.uk). Not only do they stock lots

of jewellery designers, but they also have their own
designs and will work to commission. Jess Canty, who
owns Jess James, revolutionized the jewellery industry
when he opened his shop ten years ago with his fresh
approach. None of that stuffy, scary business you normally associate with 'proper' jewellers. Although he
trades in a lot of modern silver designs, you can also
get gold, antiquey things. His ideas and designs are
innovative and classy and his shop is absolutely worth
a visit. It is cram-packed with great ideas, from the
very reasonably priced to the more expensive. Jess
does something called prayer rings, which are destined
to become new classics because they are masterpieces
of engineering – nuggets of white gold, yellow gold
and platinum which you fiddle with and swivel round.
It's not perhaps right for an engagement present but it
would make a great alternative to a wedding band.
They cost £1,200 and are worth every penny. There is
also a chunky catalogue full of photos if you want to
buy by mail order, but for (especially) anyone planning to get married a trip to London to Jess James is
highly recommended.

I need help with shoes. The real problem is in summer, as my
feet are sweaty. It's not my fault – it's genetic – we are a
family of foot-sweaters. In winter my socks and insoles look
after the problem, but I really, really want to be able to wear
lightweight summer shoes without socks or tights. I tend to
wear either plimsole-type canvas shoes with insoles and
keep washing both, or strappy sandals which give enough
draughts, plus insoles if not too hideous, though nice

sandals tend not to fit my fat feet. How can I wear standard
enclosed summer shoes? Has science come up with a solution? Do foot deodorants work? The ones I tried years ago
didn't make any difference. Are my summer outfits destined
to look elegant to the ankles and ridiculous thereafter for
ever? Help me! – *Jo Griggs, East Sussex*

I have no idea if foot deodorants work as, she says
smugly, I have never had any need for them. In fact,
my feet have always been so remarkably unsmelly that
it has caused astonishment among my friends. Once
when I was on holiday with five girlfriends we all
bought the same flat canvas shoes. Towards the end of
the holiday all theirs stunk like an incontinent tramp's
pants, but not mine. Of course, you know about the
merits of wearing footwear with leather insoles rather
than yukky perspiration-inducing synthetic (quite a
lot of the time shoes will have leather uppers and syn-
thy stuff next to your feet, which I think is quite, quite
stupid). There isn't a solution as such, just some suggestions. There will be times when you have to wear
enclosed shoes in the summer; for these times I suggest
you try the following: to stop the sweating, try a
product called Trust, which comes in a cream form in
a very small pot which lasts for ages and is, I have it on
good authority, very effective. You put it on about
twice a week – putting it on overnight and washing it
off the next morning. After that you can wash as many
times as you like without affecting it until the next
'application'. It doesn't stop you sweating but ensures
that your sweat never smells. You can get it from
places like Boots for about £8. Or, if you decide you

118 dear annie
**Secret Socks, which are awarded the second Gold
Star.** They will go some way to absorbing the sweat
and protect the shoes and you also won't need to wash
your trainers and stuff so often. You know those
hideous footlets you get that are the colour of old
ladies' knickers? Well, Secret Socks are not like that
because they are in thin towelling and are very 'discreet'. They come in black, white or beige, in sizes
small (shoe sizes 2–4), medium (4–7), large (7–9) and
extra large (10–13), and cost £2.15 per pair (mail order
and enquiries: 020 8445 5115). They wash up brilliantly and everyone should have some. Marks and Spencer
also make something called Trainer Liners which are
nicer because they stay on better but they are visible
because they come higher up the foot. They are great
for 'active wear' however, and I find them more comfy
in trainers than Secret Socks. They come in white,
black and grey and cost £5 for two. Finally, try
Sundaes (01406 371370). They make sandals to order
[see their entry in the 'Big Shoe' directory: www.dear-
annie.com], so even if your feet are 'fat', these will fit!
Finally, when you take your shoes off and they are
resting – even sandals – dust them with a bit of talc to
absorb moisture and keep them fresh.

My latest plan is a trip to Peru. The holiday notes advise a
'strong pair of walking boots'. I have never worn such a
thing and the ones I have seen in the shops are almost too
heavy to lift off the shelves, let alone attempt to lift up and
down on the end of my feet. Could you find out for me

please whether there are such things as strong but light-weight walking boots, and if so who sells them? My feet and I will be eternally grateful. – *Maggie Paul, Esher, Surrey*

I love, love, love my **Ecco boots** ('Ecco boots, far away . . . da da . . . Ecco boots far away . . . da da . . .'). Hello. Yes, they are fantastic and **holders of Gold Star numero three.** I bought mine in Street in Somerset two years ago and they are light and wonderful but also tough and high-performing, with things like Gore-Tex linings (keep your feet from getting too hot – I even wear my boots in high summer with no discomfort – yet also keep them warm in winter). I'm not even going to bother recommending anyone else, because I know just what you mean about walking boots that are so heavy you never want to put them on. Your nearest shop is the Ecco Shop, 18 White Lion Walk, Guildford, Surrey GU1 3DN, tel: 01483 302574. The stockist helpline number is 0800 387368. They are expensive (about £110 for a Gor-Tex pair) but walking boots (proper ones) are. (Ecco boots actually inspired me to introduce the Gold Star system.)

I have turned to you in desperation! My beloved digital watch has finally given out after fourteen years and I can't find another one anywhere. I'm not particularly feminine but I don't want a monstrosity of a sports one like in the shops as I have a very small wrist and hand. I also would prefer a leather strap but I could change that. The absolute biggest size I could stand is about 2cm by 2cm and, please, something tasteful! My last watch was a Timex with a light and an

alarm and something with those would be brilliant.
Otherwise, up to £50 and anywhere in the country as I have
relatives everywhere! – *Miriam Osner, Sheffield*

I find it hard to recommend anything, as digital
watches should, to my mind, be worn big and
chunky. Although Casio do some pretty nice slim
ones starting from £20; enquiries: 020 8450 9131.
Trying to mix digital displays with small, feminine
styling looks yuk to me. I'd much rather you got
yourself to Cobra and Bellamy (149 Sloane Street,
London SW1X 9BZ, tel: 020 7730 9993) and bought
yourself a lovely 'old-fashioned' watch with hands.
They do a cheapie range (but frigging gorgeous) that
starts at about the £49 mark. And here is where I
launch into a story. About five years ago I went into
Cobra and Bellamy in the course of my job, and
found the watch I had been looking for all my life. It
was silver with a long rectangular face, very Art Deco.
I was obsessed with it but it cost around £600. Every
time I spoke to Veronica (one of the owners) after
that, I asked about this masterpiece of timekeeping.
Then, about two years after I had first seen it,
Veronica rang me one day at work and said, 'Guess
what? That watch you like, we now make it in
chrome plate rather than silver and the face is curved
plastic [previously the face had been in glass and
curved glass is very difficult and expensive to pro-
duce] and it's £59.' I almost flew down there. And it is
just fabulous: it keeps time like a shop steward, is
utterly beautiful and unique, and much remarked
upon. I adore it. But this is just one watch in a

fabulous range of beautiful watches for men and
women that are beautifully styled and ridiculously
well priced; for which **Cobra and Bellamy win a
Gold Star.**

I am planning a holiday later this year and want to be able to
swim. But I have an added problem when choosing a swimsuit as I had a mastectomy last year. I have heard that there
are some companies that specialize in this area but feel
apprehensive and don't know where to start looking.
– H. Everidge, Kingston

Please don't be apprehensive. Going on holiday and
swimming are both positive steps after a mastectomy
and your attitude is to be applauded. Naturally you
don't know where to start looking because, thankfully,
this isn't an area of swimsuits that you've ever had to
worry about before. Mastectomy swimsuits have to be
cleverly thought out as they can't be too low and have
to be high-cut under the arms to conceal scarring.
[Have a good look through the 'Swimwear' directory
on my website: www.dearannie.com, for a full selection of who does mastectomy swimwear (Fantasie,
Splash Out and Rigby and Peller are three to look out
for especially, but there are others).] Someone I'm
going to recommend above all others is the excellent,
the divine, the fabulous **Margaret Ann (01985
840520), holder of Gold Star number five.** Margaret
Ann is an underwear/swimwear expert [for the full
low-down, look at 'Swimwear' and 'Underwear' directories – she is in both]. She works with lots of post-
mastectomy women and her service is superb; she has

literally changed the lives of thousands of women. She doesn't just deal with mastectomy but with larger-than-average-sized swimwear, underwear, first bras – you name it, she does it. If a bra can be got in the world, she can get it. Margaret Ann is so excellent I think she should be knighted.

My husband and I are going on a long (three-month) trip across the States and maybe further afield. It will be fairly 'adventurous' in the sense that we'll be walking lots and maybe even do some rock-climbing! We'd like to get some 'outdoor' gear like fleeces, waterproofs, etc. and need your guidance as to what makes are really good. We won't be buying loads (this isn't a trip up Everest after all) but I do want them to be good quality. I have dreadful memories of buying an inferior ski jacket one winter and freezing to death. We're only in our thirties and I HATE patterns. Hope this isn't being too fussy. – *Mr and Mrs Davies, Cornwall*

Good grief, you are not being fussy in the slightest. I *insist* on the highest-performance outdoor wear. I could have cried with frustration when fleeces (which naturally I had been wearing for ages) became . . . oh my goodness, I can barely say it . . . *fashionable.* And in the trail of this trendiness there were *fashion fleeces.* Look no further, my good woman, than my favourite, favourite label of all time: **Patagonia, Gold Star awardee number six.** I have oft joked to Mr Annie that I want to be buried wearing one of my Patagonia fleeces, but actually I rather fancy something a little smarter would be more apt. But enough of this talk. Patagonia was started in 1973 by people

who fished/climbed rocks – that type of thing. Hence
their stuff is not the cheapest, but it is superb. I can
spot a piece of Patagonia clothing from fifty paces
and it quickens my heartbeat every time. I have about
ten of their fleeces, in various weights and for various
conditions, and all are excellent. For your trip I'd
particularly recommend the Retro Cardigan (a fabulous, slightly fitted fleece with zip front) and the
Retro-X waistcoat, which is wind-proof. I also have
their silk-weight long johns and zip turtle neck, their
neck gaiters, their bags, their Bunting gloves, all their
fishing stuff . . . etc., etc. This is a cliché, but I cannot
recommend Patagonia enough – they are a class
apart. Call 0033 141101818 for their catalogue (you
can do mail order or ring that number for your nearest stockist, but I'd go the mail-order route; you'll
have a far better choice) and get drooling.
STOP PRESS! At this stage I would also like to tell
you about Maureen Smith of Splash Out who will be
awarded a gold star in the next edition of the *Dear
Annie* book. She makes swimwear to order for very
reasonable prices – read all about her in my
Swimwear directory on www.dearannie.com or ring
her direct: 01903 506677.

index

faber and faber

Amongst Women
John McGahern

Winner of the Irish Times–Aer Lingus Irish Literature Prize
for Fiction 1990
Shortlisted for the Booker Prize 1990

Moran is an old Republican whose life was transformed for
ever by his days of glory as a guerrilla leader in the War of
Independence. Now, in old age, living out in the country,
Moran is still fighting – with his family, his friends, even
himself – in a poignant struggle to come to terms with the
past.

'A masterpiece.' John Banville

'Though it bears no trace of strain, no whiff of midnight
oil, it is obviously the product of much loving labour. It is
compact but not dense, spare yet rich, and brimming with
tension.' *Observer*

faber and faber

Headlong
Michael Frayn

Shortlisted for the Booker Prize 1999

Martin Clay, a young would-be art historian, suddenly sees
opening in front of him the chance of a lifetime: the oppor-
tunity to perform a great public service, and at the same
time to make his professional reputation – perhaps even
rather a lot of money as well. To obtain the treasure he
thinks he has identified involves him setting up a classic
sting and risking everything that is valuable to him – and so
he finds himself drawn step by step into a moral and
intellectual labyrinth.

'Elegant, witty and sparklingly knowledgeable . . . there is
no doubt about the sureness of Frayn's achievement in this
black and brilliant comedy of uncertainties.' Peter Kemp,
Sunday Times

'The precision of plot is as sparkling as ever; but Frayn's dis-
section of his characters – social, intellectual, ethical – is
even more dazzling . . . Michael Frayn is outstanding.'
Caroline Moore, *Sunday Telegraph*

faber and faber

The Last King of Scotland
Giles Foden

Winner of the 1998 Whitbread First Novel Award

The Last King of Scotland is Idi Amin – just one of the many titles the Ugandan dictator awarded himself. And in the shape of young doctor Nicholas Garrigan, newly arrived in Kampala, it appears that the 'Conquerer of the British Empire' has found himself a Scottish subject.

Dark and comic by turns, based closely on historical events, **The Last King of Scotland** is a journey into the mind of the African tyrant who became a cartoon bogeyman for the rest of the world. And as a powerful meditation on the nature of charisma and corruption, Giles Foden's novel marks the emergence of a singular new talent in British fiction.

'The most accomplished debut was Giles Foden's **The Last King of Scotland**, a vivid evocation of Seventies Uganda and the "naked visceral attraction" a terrible dictator could hold for a Western liberal doctor.' John Walsh, *Independent*

'Faithfully illuminated and near-flawlessly re-created in Giles Foden's Whitbread prize-winning debut, a novel where fact and imagination are artfully intwined by the invisible thread of the author's prose . . . Foden's unnervingly convincing portraiture dominates the narrative.' *Sunday Times*

faber and faber

The Lord of the Flies
William Golding

Winner of the Nobel Prize for Literature

A plane crashes on an uninhabited island and the only survivors, a group of schoolboys, assemble on the beach and wait to be rescued. By day they inhabit a land of bright, fantastic birds and dark blue seas, but at night their dreams are haunted by the image of a terrifying beast.

In this his first novel, William Golding gave the traditional adventure story an ironic, devastating twist. The boys' delicate sense of order fades, and their childish fears are transformed into something deeper and more primitive. Their games take on a horrible significance, and before long the well-behaved party of schoolboys has turned into a tribe of faceless, murderous savages.

First published in 1954, **Lord of the Flies** is now recognised as a classic, one of the most celebrated of all modern novels.

'It begins like a Ballantyne yarn, but ends grimly otherwise. Beautifully written, tragic and provocative.' E. M. Forster

'Beautiful and desperate . . . something quite out of the ordinary.' Stevie Smith

faber and faber

Oscar and Lucinda
Peter Carey

Winner of the 1988 Booker Prize
Also a major film starring Ralph Fiennes and Cate Blanchett

Daring, original, intense and bizarre, **Oscar and Lucinda** is a
brilliant achievement – a moving love story and an historical
tour de force that is also powerfully contemporary.

'**Oscar and Lucinda** is a little like the best Australian
movie ever made, except that it is a magnificent novel in
its own right – Carey's finest achievement to date.'
Peter Porter, *Daily Telegraph*

'A novel of extraordinary richness, complexity and
strength . . . It fills me with a wild, savage envy, and no
novelist could say fairer than that.' Angela Carter, *Guardian*

faber and faber

The Poisonwood Bible
Barbara Kingsolver

Shortlisted for the Orange Prize

Told by the wife and four daughters of Nathan Price, a fierce evangelical Baptist who takes his family and mission to the Belgian Congo in 1959, **The Poisonwood Bible** is the story of one family's tragic undoing and remarkable reconstruction over the course of three decades in post-colonial Africa. They carry with them all they believe they will need from home, but soon find that all of it – from garden seeds to Scripture – is calamitously transformed on African soil.

'There are few ambitious, successful and beautiful novels. Lucky for us we have one now in **The Poisonwood Bible**.' Jane Smiley

'**The Poisonwood Bible** shows what happens when one of the most talented writers of our generation comes to maturity . . . [It] ranks with the most ambitious works of post-colonial literature and it should at last establish Kingsolver's reputation in Europe as one of America's most gifted novelists.' *Independent on Sunday*

'Brilliant. Now, that is no sort of measured critical reaction but it is how I feel I must begin – with a one-word shout of praise for this superb epic novel.' Margaret Forster, *Literary Review*

faber and faber

Red Earth and Pouring Rain
Vikram Chandra

'Chandra is imagining and writing with such originality and intensity as to be not merely drawing on myth but making it.' *Sunday Times*

'Makes its British counterparts look like apologetic throat-clearings.' Adam Thorpe

faber and faber

The Unbearable Lightness of Being
Milan Kundera

'A dark and brilliant achievement.' Ian McEwan

The Unbearable Lightness of Being is a story of irreconcil-
able love and infidelities in which Milan Kundera addresses
himself to the nature of twentieth-century 'Being', offering a
wide range of brilliant and amusing philosophical specula-
tions. First published in 1984, Kundera's masterly novel
encompasses the extremes of comedy and tragedy and
was at once hailed by critics as a contemporary classic.

'There are novels that are tragic, or entertaining, and this
one is both. There are very few that give a fresh perspec-
tive on existence, and force the reader to reassess his own
life and attitudes.' Victoria Glendinning, *Sunday Times*

Please send me

	title	ISBN	Price
_____	The New York Trilogy *Paul Auster*	15223 6	£6.99
_____	Jack Maggs *Peter Carey*	19377 3	£6.99
_____	Oscar and Lucinda *Peter Carey*	15304 6	£7.99
_____	Red Earth and Pouring Rain		
_____	*Vikram Chandra*	17456 6	£7.99
_____	Pig Tales *Marie Darrieussecq*	19372 2	£6.99
_____	Hullabaloo in the Guava Orchard		
_____	*Kiran Desai*	19571 7	£6.99
_____	The Last King of Scotland *Giles Foden*	19564 4	£6.99
_____	Headlong *Michael Frayn*	20147 4	£6.99
_____	Lord of the Flies *William Golding*	19147 9	£6.99
_____	The Remains of the Day *Kazuo Ishiguro*	15491 3	£6.99
_____	The Unconsoled *Kazuo Ishiguro*	17754 9	£7.99
_____	The Poisonwood Bible *Barbara Kingsolver*	20175 X	£7.99
_____	Immortality *Milan Kundera*	14456 X	£7.99
_____	The Unbearable Lightness of Being		
_____	*Milan Kundera*	13539 0	£6.99
_____	The Buddha of Suburbia *Hanif Kureishi*	14274 5	£6.99
_____	Aunt Julia and the Scriptwriter		
_____	*Mario Vargas Llosa*	16777 2	£7.99
_____	Amongst Women *John McGahern*	16160 X	£6.99
_____	A Fine Balance *Rohinton Mistry*	17936 3	£7.99
_____	Birds of America *Lorrie Moore*	19727 2	£6.99
_____	Our Fathers *Andrew O'Hagan*	20106 7	£6.99
_____	The Bell Jar *Sylvia Plath*	08178 9	£6.99

**To order these titles phone Bookpost on 01624 836000
Or complete the order form below:**

I enclose a cheque for £ _____ made payable to Bookpost PLC
Please charge my: o Mastercard   o Visa   o Amex   o Delta
o Switch   Switch Issue No _____

Credit Card No _____ Expiry date _____

Name _____

Address _____

_____ Postcode _____

Signed _____ Date _____

Free postage and packing in the UK.
Overseas customers allow £1 per pbk/ £3 per hbk.
Send to: Bookpost PLC, PO Box 29, Douglas, Isle of Man, IM99 1BQ
fax: 01624 837033 email: bookshop@enterprise.net
http://www.bookpost.co.uk